THE MONOPOLY OF CREDIT

Errata:
1. Front cover page, commentary, line 5 should read "the causes of War", etc.
2. Introduction, p. xxii, last line should read "the European Economic Community."
3. Contents, p. xxix, Chapter I should read "Government by Finance", etc.

Books by C. H. Douglas:

Economic Democracy
Credit Power and Democracy
The Control and Distribution of Production
Social Credit
Warning Democracy
The Alberta Experiment
These Present Discontents and the Labour Party
The New and the Old Economics
The Big Idea
The "Land for the (Chosen) People" Racket
Programme for the Third World War
"Whose Service is Perfect Freedom"
The Brief for the Prosecution

Addresses and Essays (Pamphlets) by C. H. Douglas:

Social Credit Principles
Reconstruction
The Use of Money
The Nature of Democracy
Money and the Price System
The Approach to Reality
The Tragedy of Human Effort
Security: Institutional and Personal
The Policy of a Philosophy
This "American" Business
Realistic Constitutionalism
The Realistic Position of the Church of England

THE MONOPOLY OF CREDIT

BY

C. H. DOUGLAS

Fourth (Douglas Centenary) Edition
with an introduction
by Geoffrey Dobbs

BLOOMFIELD BOOKS
26 Meadow Lane,
SUDBURY,
Suffolk, ENGLAND, CO10 6TD
1979

First Edition 1931
First Edition–second impression 1933
Second (revised and enlarged) Edition 1937
Third (revised) Edition 1951
Third (revised) Edition–reprinted 1958
Fourth (Douglas Centenary) Edition 1979

The Fourth Edition consists of the text of the Third Edition with the addition of an Introduction by Geoffrey Dobbs, an Index, and Notes about the Author.

ISBN: 0 904656 01 2 Paperback
        0 904656 02 0 Hardback

Published by:
    Bloomfield Books,
    26 Meadow Lane, SUDBURY,
    Suffolk, ENGLAND, CO10 6TD.

Overseas agents:

Heritage Publications,
273 Little Collins Street, MELBOURNE,
Victoria, AUSTRALIA, 3000.

Canadian Intelligence Publications,
Box 130, FLESHERTON,
Ontario, CANADA, NOC 1EO.

Conservative Publications,
P.O. Box 736, TAURANGA,
NEW ZEALAND.

Dolphin Press (Pty) Ltd.,
P.O. Box 1564, KRUGERSDORP,
Transvaal, SOUTH AFRICA, 1740.

PREFACE TO
THE THIRD EDITION

SINCE this book was first published, at a time when the Anglo-Saxon world was shivering from financial and economic depression (only ended by re-armament for the second War-phase), there has been a shift, more apparent than real, from rule by finance to rule by Order-in-Council. To anyone who will take the trouble to analyse the course of events, however, it must be obvious that the Monopoly of Credit, which means the effective domination of human activity, is being pursued with relentless persistence.

On the outcome of this policy, so far as can be seen, depends the earthly destiny of the human race.

C. H. DOUGLAS

FEARNAN, PERTHSHIRE.
June, 1950.

ARGUMENT

How is it possible for a world which is suffering from over-production to be in economic distress? Where does money come from? Why should we economise when we are making too many goods? How can an unemployment problem, together with a manufacturing and agricultural organisation which cannot obtain orders, exist side by side with a poverty problem? Must we balance our budget? Why should we be asked to have confidence in our money system, if it works properly?

It is hoped that answers to these and similar questions will be suggested by a perusal of the following pages.

INTRODUCTION

IT is appropriate that this book should be republished during the centenary year of the author's birth. It is necessary, however, to remind the reader that it was first published in 1931, at the beginning of what is now known as The Great Depression, and has not been more than minimally revised since 1937. The author's last Preface, to this Third Edition, written in 1950 and here reprinted, drew attention to: "a shift, more apparent than real, from rule by finance to rule by Orders in Council". But it is since then that the major acceleration of the changes implicit in the main thesis of the book and its predecessors has taken place. Hence the advisability of this Introduction.

The first of these changes is the establishment of worldwide, universal price inflation as a permanent built-in feature of the world's monetary system, common to both socialist and capitalist or mixed economies. There is no question any longer of price stability or of a general fall in prices, whatever the advances in technology, or the restrictions on credit; the only question concerns the rate of price inflation, even during a trade depression. This disposes conclusively of the superficial criticism that used to be made of Douglas's analysis, that he had mistaken a temporary aberration, during the 1930's, due to an excessive measure of deflation, for a permanent feature of the monetary system.

A second major change has been the growth of what used to be a quite minor form of "instalment buying", instituted during the 1930's, into a massive and quite essential factor in the economy, without which it would collapse. In the most advanced economy, that of the U.S.A., various forms of "credit purchase", particularly those using the innumerable "credit cards", have now ousted normal, cash, or cheque, payment as the main means of buying. A more conclusive proof of the time lag between prices and incomes which is the essence of Douglas's economic thesis it is difficult to imagine.

A third major development in the situation is the growth of bureaucracy and of Government control over the lives of the citizens, whether by means of finance or by direct regulation and licensing, until much more than half the economy is now either directly in the "public sector" or in partial or indirect control through Government nominees or agents. Nationalisation, which was to have brought about a socialist Utopia of selfless public service, has brought only disillusionment and bitter disputes about money, at enormous cost and injury to the public. Nationalisation of the Bank of England which, according to many monetary reformers, was to have ensured the "democratic control" of the monetary system, has merely conferred political status on the credit monopoly.

In recent years, it has been notorious that many businesses, including some of the highest technical efficiency and reputation, have been quite unable to recover their costs by sales to the public and, if deemed important enough, have had to be "rescued" from bankruptcy by the Government, which can raise its borrowing requirement because it has the power to recover the loan by compulsory taxation. This means that instead of the involuntary "price subsidy" provided, as Douglas points out, by the sale of bankrupt stock below cost, we now have sales below cost subsidised by Government credits which place a further burden of future taxes upon the public. Indeed, it has now become axiomatic that it is impossible for the bulk of the public to pay out of income or credit for major services such as those of health or education, however much money these services disburse in wages. Whole industries cannot now be expected to pay their way without Government aid, and the proportion of the national product which the citizens' incomes are capable of buying, other than through compulsory taxes, is continually falling, both in size and in quality.

It is a significant confirmation of Douglas's thesis that the basis for financial credit is progressively shifting from normal trading (i.e. the capacity to create wealth and recover the loan with interest by selling to the public) to the power of the State to extract money by force. The failure of the attempts of recent

Governments of both major Parties to "fight inflation" by supressing price rises by force of law, and wage increases similarly or by negotiation with the Trades Union Congress, has merely illustrated the inanity of trying to "fight" arithmetic. If wages cannot meet prices without mortgaging the future, and prices cannot cover escalating costs unless they also are allowed to "escalate", no amount of repressive force from the State can make them do so. The most that can be achieved has been a temporary reduction in the rate of price inflation, accompanied by universal discontent and frustration, and followed by a price and wage "explosion" when the pressure is relieved. Attempts then to control this by monetary restriction merely depress the whole economy and increase the frustrated demands for "more money" and "more employment", which only the State can provide.

The monetary time-trap in which we are all caught is driving every Western nation, irrespective of its political ideology, towards State Socialism, with its dependence upon the State as the source of all access to wealth and power, and this superficially appears to confirm the Marxist view that there is a fatal defect inherent in what is called capitalist free enterprise which spells its doom and drives it inexorably towards socialism. The necessity to maximise exports, not to barter for essential imports, but to provide pay-packets to buy home products without adding to the price-income gap, is also forcing the "mixed economies" of the West to support with their still superior technology the grossly inefficient economies of the Socialist East and even, suicidally, to enable them to gain a preponderance in arms.

Indeed, there could be no better way of forcing people into a state of fury and frustration, leading to revolution and chaos and finally to submission with relief to dictatorship, than for virtually all Governments, parties, churches and other major influences to strive continually to mould human nature, human lives and human institutions into whatever shapes are variously believed to be capable of minimising the injustices implicit in the rules of mathematics; without even a glance at the massive evidence that those rules are being misapplied to society in the usages of our monetary debt system.

At the time I am writing this (August 1979) the wheel seems to have come round almost full circle to the situation when *The Monopoly of Credit* was written at the beginning of the 1930's. Then it was a National Government which was telling us here in Great Britain that we must return to "sound finance" and live within our monetary means, and that the cure for our indigence must be to cut down our work and wealth production and waste everything that we could not afford to buy. The insanity of that approach to a situation of manifest "poverty in plenty" was obvious to most people, even at the time; but now a similar, but even more extreme situation is wrapped up somewhat differently.

An electorate disillusioned with socialism has once more installed a Conservative Government, this time pledged to turn back the tide of bureaucracy and Government spending and to rely again on "market forces" which, however, cannot be left "free" to achieve our real capacity, but must be firmly controlled within our approved financial "means" by monetary restriction. In other words, the recipe as before—which can only demonstrate again that what is miscalled "free enterprise" under time-lag financing does not "work" without cumulative frustrations which call for progressive Government interference.

The difference this time is that, whereas in the 1930's monetary restriction at least temporarily halted the devaluation of the currency, now, nearly half a century later, it can cause no more than a hiccup in the rate of inflation. It is true that under "capitalism", forced bankruptcies and the proliferation of various forms of credit purchasing may somewhat postpone the day of reckoning, but there are limits to these and when they are reached there remains one final resort only for those engaged in a persistent attempt to achieve the mathematically impossible, namely compulsion: a power wielded only by monopolies. And the final monopoly in the matter of financial compulsion is the power of taxation by the State; which brings us back to some form of "socialism", whatever Government is in power.

In the course of quite extensive contacts with academic economists of the Left, the Right and the Centre, I have long ago come to the conclusion that it is virtually impossible for any mind which has accepted the axioms implicit in first-year Economics to come to grips at all with the realistic thinking of an engineer such as Douglas. The concept of the real credit: the capacity to make and deliver what is wanted, as, when and where it is wanted, which is basic to the production of anything for sale to the public, is quite inconceivable and unreal to an economist unless it incorporates the account-ancy arrangement called money, which, despite its well-known and wholly symbolic nature, is still credited with the properties of a real entity—a commodity such as gold, for instance —of which there can be a quantity, a stock, a store. Upon this illusory basis the whole vast and subtle structure of economic thought has been built, so that there is no escape from cir-cular thinking. An actual capacity to produce, or a need and want for the product, cannot be made effective without money; hence they have no "reality" for economists except in monetary terms. And since practically all economic concepts, however complex or abstract, incorporate this idea of money as if it were a neutral "unit of account", "medium of exchange", "measure and store of value" and so forth, the possibility is eliminated *ab initio* of comparing the economics which is determined by the nature and use of bank credit with that which could exist if the accountancy were secondary, and not a determining factor.

Another result of this treatment of money as if it were a simple "quantity" is that the polarity in respect of time which is introduced by its creation, not as a simple quantity addition, but always as a repayable loan, is ignored. Although individuals and businesses have to balance their debits and their credits, when it comes to the economy as a whole, units of account are totted up whether they are coming or going, on the plus or minus side of the debt ledger, whether they are cancelling costs or creating them. Thus, when economists have added up all the borrowed mortgage-money paid out to maintain witless, useless, redundant, unwanted, destructive, or simply irrelevant "employment", they find that there is "too much money chasing too few" of the miserable trickle of wanted and needed goods and services actually produced and allowed to reach the consumer. They then cannot understand how permanent and progressive inflation, quite as much as the deflation of the 1930's, is a sign of a progressive time-lag in the generation of incomes as compared with prices, which can be neutralised only by a direct issue of credit to the consumer (whether by dividend or price discount, or both).

However much it is sophisticated, the argument is essentially the simple one that, if inflation is due to too much of a homogeneous quantitative entity called "money", to add more "money" will make it worse. But "money" is not a homogeneous entity, it is a loan, which is travelling either outward, creating debt, or inward, cancelling it. The best analogy is, perhaps, a chemical one. A state of inflation might be compared to one of corrosive acid poisoning, due to a gross excess of (positive, hydrogen) ions. The urgent need is to neutralise these with a base, i.e. by adding negative, basic, ions. The argument that, since the damage is due to an excess of "ions", to add more "ions" would make it worse, is quite analogous with that used by economists who reject Douglas's analysis and proposals as "inflationary".

The advance of technology, since this book was last printed, has radically changed the world picture so as to reinforce the urgency of its main thesis. The silicon chip or "micro-processor" revolution has introduced a new quality and acceleration into the displacement of human by non-human "employment"; but so far no accepted party or school of thought has faced the realities which were demonstrated by Douglas half a century ago. The universal need for pay packets still imposes the perverse aim of using such liberating devices to "make more work"; and the "higher" the technology, the longer the series of electronic, mechanical, or other power-devices used in the "work", the greater the time-lag between the distribution of the "pay" and of the consumable product (if any).

All human work necessarily consumes energy

and materials, which are wasted if the product is not consumed or used by people in some beneficial way. "Waste" and "pollution" are merely names given to products which are not so used, or are actually detrimental; and these are maximised to the extent that production is controlled primarily by monetary objectives (jobs and profits) or by centralised planning imposed upon the consumer, instead of the pay and profits being the automatic measure of the satisfaction of consumer demand. Consumption itself, of imposed or inferior products in response to an artificially created "demand", can include a large element of waste or pollution, e.g. excessive eating, drinking, smoking or remedy-taking, or the buying of prestige-gadgetry; and the often-quoted objective of creating new "wants", even "necessities" for mankind so that many people shall "earn their livings" supplying them, reveals the current perversion of economic policy.

The progressive magnification of waste and pollution has now produced its reaction in the self-styled Ecology Movement. This, I am convinced, began as a very genuine and long overdue warning and protest against the squandering of the earth's resources, the destruction of life, and the mauling and pollution of environment which are the inescapable accompaniments of the attempt to provide "work for all" in the face of rapid technological advance, for the purpose of distributing money. Unfortunately the "Ecologists" have not pursued their analysis far enough, and the psychological background they have created of vanishing energy sources and a soon-starving planet has been found all too useful by those who have a permanent interest in "scarce resources" and in the maintenance of permanent "economic crisis" as a justification for draconic measures of "control". Plenty is, by definition, excluded from economics; and the aphorism, attributed to Professor Milton Friedman, that "There is no such thing as a free lunch" indicates that, if such a thing threatens, the approved "economic" treatment is to throw it away, plough it in, or spoil it for human consumption with a dye, which depicts, roughly, the agricultural policy adopted by European Economic Community.

It is true enough that the continued debt-financing of "work for all" in a technological age is the way to impoverish the planet and bring the much-prophesied "doom" upon mankind; though in view of the resilience of nature, and of human nature, this could scarcely be achieved without ruthless determination and perverse ingenuity and persistence in large-scale, organised interference with vital and regenerative processes. It is also true that the anticipation of real scarcity is invaluable as a "cover" for the imposition of blatantly political "shortages" (e.g. the current "oil crisis") with artificially inflated prices, which in turn stimulate ever more extravagant efforts to extract and use up "scarce resources". Only, for instance, against a background of "crisis" and "energy scarcity" can a deeply suspicious public be persuaded to accept nuclear power as a major source of energy generation.

The nuclear power station, as judged by the claims of its advocates rather than of its opponents, offers the most extreme physical expression to date of the take-now-pay-later principle embodied in our financial and economic system. Its immensely expensive "fuel", the product of elaborate technological processes of extraction and refinement, is "used" in electricity generation to the extent of about 1 per cent. It can be handled only by remote control, and the public is assured that it is "the safest form of energy" because it is subjected to layer upon layer upon layer and check upon check of complicated technical safety precautions which are required by no other form of energy generation. The life of a nuclear power station is a very few decades; and the "spent fuel" remains as a "hot waste" which then requires vitrefying, burying at great depth in carefully selected sites, and after that "monitoring" for an indefinite time, according to the lowest estimates at least for some centuries to come. Payment on the "never-never" indeed!

Without entering upon the beaten path of the "nuclear" controversy, the point I want to make here is that the price of nuclear energy, at the point of use and of sale, is far below its cost, both real and financial. In this it resembles the products of all large-scale, capital-intensive, centralised undertakings dependent upon government borrowing and taxation for development. The nuclear energy so far available is known to be a sequel to the development of the A-bomb or fission-bomb, but the probability now looms that the enormously greater energy developed in the H-bomb or fusion-bomb may be brought under control within a generation or so. At present, we are assured, these immense forces are arrayed in banks of inter-continental missiles, threatening the instant obliteration of a large proportion of mankind.

It is a strange world in which "astronomical" credits have been forthcoming to enable energy to be organised in this way—also to surround the earth with hundreds of orbiting satellites, to send men to the Moon and scientific probes to explore the nearer planets—while the population is threatened with "energy shortage", and even with widespread starvation and a general shortage of everything.

If fusion-reactors eventually become practicable, it will be at tremendous, and inflationary, capital cost, and the energy provided will be even more centralised than at present, placing huge populations in dependence upon the demands of a handful of men. In contrast, the greatest "fusion-reactor" of all, the Sun, still pours its continual stream of energy in decentralised form upon the whole planet, providing "burdensome surpluses" of food wherever there is a profitable monetary return, as well as indirect sources of energy in wind and water. The carefully fostered idea of an intrinsic, material poverty of the planet is the reverse of the truth. The issue is one of policy, between centralised and decentralised control of the energy and resources of the earth, and it is quite clear that if the control of financial credit is ignored, the confrontations of contemporary politics are quite irrelevant to it.

Credit is not a material thing; it belongs to the world of the mind and spirit, of the faith even more than the intellect. Money, a form of power, has always been associated with some corruption in so far as it has been centralised, though while it had a physical form it was somewhat limited by the laws of nature. When it became wholly abstract—a numerical artifact originating in a particular category of men—

this limitation was removed. A return to a link with a single easily monopolised commodity such as gold would not decentralise the power of credit monopoly. This would require what Douglas proposes, that financial credit should be based upon real credit, and not upon an arbitrary currency, and should be correctly distributed to the public.

Such a reversal of policy is a challenge to the unconscious objectives, rather than the technical knowledge, of professional economists, who are unable to admit in plain words what is implicit in their technical language. Keynes and his followers, for instance, who created the mental background for continuous economic "growth" and inflation, never acknowledged that these had become the built-in requirements of our credit-and-employment system. And the currently fashionable Monetarists, whose very name implies their advocacy of the manipulation of the economy by the central control of the money supply, will never admit that there is a Monopoly of Credit. Proposals which were ridiculed when first put forward by Douglas, such as "social incomes", consumer credits, and sales below cost at credit-compensated prices, are now being massively applied in inverted fashion, so as to postpone and aggravate, rather than to cancel, the deficiency to which he drew attention, and to centralise further, rather than to decentralise, the control of credit.

God only knows what disasters the world will have to endure before our rulers, or some of them, will open their minds to the truth contained in this book, which, it seems, presents too penetrating a perspective to be seen by preoccupied and clever men. But whatever happens, the more people can escape from the hypnotic Left/Right dialectical two-step on the Marxist one-way street to look at something more fundamental, the more hope there must be for an eventual triumph of sanity.

Geoffrey Dobbs

Bangor, North Wales,
August 1979

CONTENTS

CHAPTER I

GOVERNMENT BY FINANCE

It cannot have escaped the observation of anyone interested in the welfare and orderly progress of society that, more especially in the years which have intervened since the close of the European War and the present time, the centre of gravity of world affairs has shifted from Parliaments and Embassies to Bank Parlours and Board Rooms. It is probable that this shifting is more apparent than real; that, in fact, Parliaments and Embassies have not for a long time been more than the salesmen of policies which were manufactured elsewhere. But the public is becoming increasingly dissatisfied with the goods; it has changed the window-dressers with disappointing results, and in consequence it is, perhaps for the first time, beginning to take an interest in matters of economics and finance which previously it had been content to leave to experts.

1

One of the first results of this awakening interest has been a demonstration of the distance which separates exact knowledge from popular understanding of the methods by which the ordinary necessities of life and the amenities of civilised existence are placed at the disposal of individuals in the modern world. If this ignorance were of a purely negative nature, the situation would be sufficiently disquieting.   But unfortunately that is not the case.   Particularly in regard to finance, which may be termed the nerve system of distribution, most people hold, with some persistence, ideas which are both incorrect and misleading, and are supported in their disinclination to change these views by sectional interests of great potency and ability in the attainment of their own objectives, which superficially seem well served by the prevailing ignorance.

No just appreciation of this situation is possible which does not take into consideration the peculiar and perhaps unique, position occupied by finance in the organisation of modern society in every country.   Finance, i.e. money, is the starting-point of every action which requires either the co-operation of the community or the use of its assets. If it be realised that control of its mechanism gives, to a major extent, control of both personal and organised activity, it is easy to see that education, publicity, and organised Intelligence (in the sense in which the word "Intelligence" is used in military circles) can be controlled, first to minimise the likelihood of criticism arising, and should it arise, depriving it of all the normal facilities for effective action. Finance can and does control policy, and as has been well said by an American writer, Charles Ferguson,[1] "control of credit and control of the news are concentric."

The results of this state of affairs can be seen somewhat sharply defined in the case of professional economists, necessarily in the direct or indirect employ of banks or insurance companies.

It would, of course, be improper and probably unfair to attribute anything but intellectual honesty to these gentlemen. Moreover, such an assumption would deny due appreciation

[1] " Revolution Absolute."

to the ability of their patrons. Their failure to make any noticeable contribution to the solution of the problems within their special field can, I think, be explained by the incompatibility of any effective solution with the credit monopoly which is at once their employer and critic.

The control of publicity renders it easy to circumscribe the reputation of the unorthodox. Modern organised publicity in its various forms is a product of costly machinery and is controlled by financial mechanism, so that, in general, any information circulated through such agencies is orthodox, while any authority recognised and advertised is a witness for the defence of things as they are, or as those at present in control of finance would desire them to be. It is therefore perhaps not astonishing that public opinion is in much the stage of economic enlightenment that we should expect as the result of the suppression and distortion of the essential facts. Most features of the social system, and many things which are not features of the social system, have in turn been blamed for its defects, with the exception of

4

the money system.   These alleged causes have been in the nature of private privileges, and it has not been difficult to manipulate popular clamour, or indeed to finance it, so as to cause the transfer of the privileges to an international plutocracy, under cover of their transfer to "the public" or "the nation".

Unable effectively to isolate the cause of the trouble, a large section of the general public, while recognising the increasing gravity of social maladjustment, has fallen back on the assumption that human nature is at fault—a comfortable theory which, while excusing the necessity for further mental effort, goes some distance towards assuring popularity in circles well able to reward it.

While all the more immediate difficulties which threaten us are in the nature of technical defects, requiring for their adjustment rather a change of head than a change of heart, it is unwise to under-estimate the psychological obstacles which lie in the path of reconstruction.   Probably that of fear is the most fundamental, fear of the unknown, fear of one's neighbour.   The psychological process known as rationalisation clothes this fear in a number of moral forms, for instance, that it is immoral that John Smith should receive goods without working although I myself receive dividends.

Economic analysis, and still more, any constructive proposal, which does not at the same time envisage the dynamics of society is unlikely to achieve more than temporary success. The Greek word from which "economics" is derived, meaning household management, is much closer to the reality of the matter than the bloodless "inexorable economic laws" which are at once the propaganda and the nightmare of the international financier; laws which, in the main, are merely the statement of the results which accrue from the operation of a purely artificial money and accountancy system.

It should be recognised clearly that minority interests have acquired, and intend to retain, all the mechanisms of organised force of which the State disposes.

The problem which faces the world, therefore, is not merely to recognise in Finance the major cause of its distress, but to devise means through which sufficient force may be brought to bear upon those agencies which alone can rectify the situation.

CHAPTER II

THE MEANING OF DISARMAMENT

PERHAPS the first step to an appreciation of the forces active in the modern world is to be gained by a consideration of the decline of moral religion.

It is easy to recognise the conflict of two systems of thought in many spheres of action, and not least in that of industry. Beyond question, the economic system which is dominated by the financial structure of banks and insurance companies is an unofficial and temporarily all-powerful government, neither elected nor subject to effective criticism, the embodiment of the concept that externally imposed restraint is the first condition of a stable society. The idea which is rising into prominence, and which is probably incompatible with the older conception, is that nations and races to some extent resemble individuals. A period of tutelage is necessary and desirable,

9

but the extension of this period beyond pragmatic limits can only result in harm and discontent. On the other hand, to say that all peoples, or even all individuals, should be suddenly freed from the restraints imposed upon them by past generations is as absurd as to say that such restraints should be uniform and permanent.

The subject is of course both wide and deep, but for the purposes of the present analysis, it may be brought down to earth by emphasising its connection with English Common Law, which again, rests on the tradition of a millenium deriving its main principles from European Christianity, grafted onto Saxon custom.

Financial civilisation, to coin a phrase of doubtful homogeneity, rests on a different legal and moral system, primarily that of the so-called Old Testament.

Whether we consider the present state of society to arise from inertia and fear, or from a positive craving for power, the recognition of its existence suggests that those who embody it will be found engaged in a struggle for the control of social forces. This, I think, is the case, and in one form or another this struggle is similar to that which has taken place throughout recorded history. The prize may be termed the unearned increment of association.

It appears to be a fundamental instinct of conscious life, well developed even in the animal kingdom, that certain advantages can be gained by the association of individuals into a group, which cannot be attained in other ways. It is equally true that in a primitive state of existence the advantages of the group carry with them definite disadvantages to the individual. It is true that many hands make light work, but it is not less true that he travels the fastest who travels alone. The developments of modern industrial society, founded upon the division of labour and co-ordinated by the financial system, have at one and the same time increased this unearned increment of association, and still further subordinated the individual to the group. Only recently has it been recognised that the factor introduced into the progress of the industrial arts by the

11

use of mechanical power in its various forms is a development not merely of degree but of kind. The advantages of the group can, as it were, be crystallised in machinery, and the human individuals receive their benefits while regaining the freedom of initiative, which has been temporarily surrendered.

While this is potentially true, it is very far from being actually so. The ingenious and subtle mechanism of the money system has obtained control of this unearned increment of association, and the modern struggle which has taken the place of the struggle for the leadership of armies is a financial struggle, with the industrial system and the world population which is dependent on it passive victims of the conflict.

The similarity of this situation to that existing in the conflict between absolute and relative morals is close. Unrestrained by the financial system, the resources of modern production would be sufficient to provide for the material desires of the whole population of the world at the expense of a small and decreasing amount of human labour. But the release of

12

humanity from the necessity of toil would also mean their release from industrial government, a result so undesired by the governors that production for the sake of consumption is becoming the least important objective of industry. The misdirection of an economic mechanism to purposes to which, from its inherent nature, it does not lend itself, is the direct, and, it would appear, fundamental explanation of the phenomena from which the world is now suffering. To say that bankers and financiers are intellectually incapable of appreciating their own problems does not, I think, provide an explanation of the purposive nature of the arrangements which the financial system is perfecting in every country; and, while contact with the more public figures of finance seems in many cases to induce surprise at the contrast between the halo and the hallowed, it must be remembered that all the brains in the world which can be bought with money are at the disposal of the banking system.

On the other hand, it is doubtless a misconception to accuse financiers of deliberately planning wars, suicide waves, bankruptcies, and the many other tragedies associated with the existing state of affairs. They are in much the position of the immoderate drinker, whom it would be absurd to suppose desires *delirium tremens*. He will do everything possible to avoid *delirium tremens*—except stop drinking.

Since it cannot be expected that this annexation of the whole harvest of human invention and endeavour can be carried out without protest, the essentially military nature of the situation becomes evident. The existing financial executive, granted that intellectual and executive capacity of which it certainly disposes, must visualise a radical conflict of objective, and the strategy applicable to this situation is similar to that of any other power whose authority is challenged. The disarmament of its adversaries, and the concentration under its own control of irresistible forces, would appear to be primary necessities.

This disarmament is in the first place of a military character. It is probable that in the modern world there is only one force superior to that of finance, and that is military force; and the best brains of the financial system are

14

well aware that whatever institutions may be saved from the next war, the present financial system will not be one of them.

Disarmament in a military sense, therefore, is a pressing requisite to a continuation of the present ascendancy of the banking system, and the sentimental pacifist is a valuable tool in its attainment. But the objective is centralisation of power, and economic disarmament is also a component of such a policy, since, while a high standard of living does not necessarily conflict with a world hegemony of finance, it is essential that the power to punish any sign of recalcitrancy on the part of the individual should exist. Personal property in the old sense seems incompatible with the objective, which contemplates the reduction of the individual to a state of powerlessness in comparison with the preponderance of a group organisation controlling the world, with omnipotent and irresponsible financiers at the head of it. The attack on personal property, which superficially would appear to proceed from the less fortunate strata of society, would never have become effective had it not been a perfect

15

tool for the transfer of real property, both territorial and industrial, from the individual to the financial institution.

CHAPTER III

THE modern State is an unlimited liability corporation, of which the citizens are the workers and guarantors, and the financial system the beneficiary. To see that this is a plain statement of fact, it is, I think, only necessary to understand the nature and the origin of money.

Money is essentially an order system. It has been defined by Professor Walker[1] as "any medium no matter of what it is made or why people want it, no one will refuse in exchange for his goods." That is to say, a given denomination of money may at any time be exchanged for any article bearing a price figure corresponding to this denomination of money, and it is a simple extension of this proposition to say that the power of creating money is a

[1] "Money, Trade and Industry," p. 6.

17

guarantee of the power of acquiring goods or services to a total proportion of the whole stock of goods and services equal to the percentage of existing money which can be created.

It is now fairly well understood that the power of creating money is for all practical purposes confined to the financial system, which is mainly under the control of the banks. Mr. McKenna, Chairman of the Midland Bank, put the matter shortly in his annual addresses to the shareholders of that institution by remarking that "every bank loan and every purchase of securities by a bank creates a deposit, and the withdrawal of every bank loan, and the sale of securities by a bank, destroys a deposit."[1] It may be noted in passing, that this is the same thing as saying that a bank acquires securities for nothing, in the same way that a central bank, such as the Bank of England, may be said to acquire gold for nothing. In each case, of course, the institution concerned writes a draft upon itself for the sum involved, and the general public

[1] Annual General Meeting, Midland Bank, January 25th, 1924.

18

honours the draft by being willing to provide goods and services in exchange for it.

Since the mechanism by which money is created by banks is not generally understood, and the subject is obviously of the highest importance, it may be well to repeat here an explanation of the matter which I have given elsewhere.

Imagine a new bank to be started—its so-called capital is immaterial. Ten depositors each deposit £100 in bank-notes with this bank. Its liabilities to the public are now £1,000. These ten depositors have business with each other and find it more convenient in many cases to write notes (cheques) to the banker, instructing him to adjust their several accounts in accordance with these business transactions, rather than to draw out cash and pay it over personally. After a little while, the banker notes that only about 10 per cent of his business is done in cash (in England it is only 0.7 of 1 per cent), the rest being merely bookkeeping. At this point depositor No. 10, who is a manufacturer, receives a large order for his product. Before he can deliver, he realises that he will have to pay out, in wages, salaries, and other expenses, considerably more " money" than he has at command. In this difficulty he consults his banker, who, having in mind the situation just outlined, agrees to allow him to draw from his account not merely his own £100 but an "overdraft" of £100, making £200 in all, in consideration of repayment in, say, three months, of £102. This overdraft of £100 is a credit to the account of depositor No. 10, who can now draw £200.

The banker's liabilities to the public are now £1,100; none of the original depositors have had their credits of £100 each reduced by the transaction, nor were they consulted in regard to it; and it is absolutely correct to say that £100 of new money has been created by a stroke of the banker's pen.

Depositor No. 10 having happily obtained his overdraft, pays it out to his employees in wages and salaries. These wages and salaries, together with the banker's interest, all go into costs. All costs go into the price the public pays for its goods, and consequently, when depositor No. 10 repays his banker with £102 obtained from the public in exchange for his goods, and the banker after placing £2, originally created by himself, to his profit and loss account, sets the £100 received against the phantom credit previously created, and cancels both of them, there are £100 worth more goods in the world which are immobilised— of which no one, not even the banker, except potentially, has the money equivalent. A short mathematical proof of this process is given in Appendix I, page 138.

Leaving for the moment certain serious difficulties of a technical nature which arise out of this process, it is, I think, desirable to examine its fundamental meaning, and a clearer idea of this may, perhaps, be obtained by considering, for example, Great Britain as a commercial undertaking and producing a balance sheet. Speaking generally, it is true to say that in any undertaking its potentialities are its assets, and the actual or contingent calls upon these potentialities are its liabilities. The subjoined balance sheet is constructed in accordance with this conception.

21

GREAT BRITAIN LTD.

Assets	*Liabilities*
(Population. Education. Morale) i.e. Human Potential.	National Debt.
Policy	Bankers (Potential creators of effective demand).
Organisation.	
Natural Resources.	Insurance Companies (Mortgage and Bondholders).
Developed Power.	
Plant (Railways, Buildings, Tools, etc.).	Cash at call.
	Taxation for Public Services.
Public Services.	
Goodwill (Tradition, reputation, etc.).	
Work in Progress.	
Consumable Goods.	

An examination of a document constructed on these principles will at once reveal the fact that it differs in certain important particulars from any official or public account. The liabilities are not defined, the fixed assets appear on the opposite side of the account to the money assets, and the two sides do not balance, and cannot, in fact, be made to balance. In short, the financial system is seen to be, as it is, in opposition to every other interest.

The assets can be generalised as the progress which the population by its individual and collective exertions has made towards the control of its environment. The liabilities are all in a form which limit this control. If a man has eight hours a day at his disposal for unspecified purposes, there is a very real sense in which his control over his environment is limited if, let us say, two out of those eight hours are required for certain services imposed upon him by the community; and, to the extent that the holders of any of the items shown on the liability side of the preceding account are in a position to call upon the community for goods and services to satisfy them, they may be considered to be a limitation of the power of the community to pursue its own ends.

These considerations inevitably involve an examination and definition of the fundamental basis of credit. Credit obviously cannot be based upon a liability, nor can the collective interests, which we call national, be so opposed to the interests of the individuals composing them that the nearer the nation approaches bankruptcy, the richer become its constituent parts. If there were no other arguments, and there are many, I think this would be sufficient to dispose of the primary contention of the existing banking and financial system, which bases credit upon currency, and in the case of Gold Standard countries, in theory, bases currency upon gold.

Real credit may be defined as the rate at which goods and services can be delivered as, when, and where required. Financial credit may similarly be defined as the rate at which money can be delivered, as, when, and where required. The inclusion in both definitions of the word "rate" is, of course, important.

An aspect of this matter worthy of attention is the convention by which the liability of the community becomes the asset of the individual. If we take the National Debt of Great Britain as being in round figures £8,000,000,000 it would be, I suppose, admitted without much hesitation that Great Britain as a community was poorer by the amount of this debt. On the other hand, each holder of War Loan would regard himself as being richer by the amount of the War Loan which he holds. Both of these statements are, of course, true, and if the Debt were held equally by individuals it would simply represent a licence to work, using National Real Capital. But the debt having been originally created by the same process which enables the banking system to create money, and so far as it is in the hands of the public, exchanging this debt so created for purchasing power already in existence, it is a transfer of purchasing power from the public to the banks. It is probable that the amount of War Debt actually owned by individuals has never exceeded 20 per cent of the total debt created, the remaining 80 per cent being either in the actual ownership, or under lien to banks and insurance companies, the net result of the

25

complete process being the transfer to the financial system of 4/5 of the purchasing power represented by £8,000,000,000.

It is no answer to this accusation to say that financial institutions are owned by individuals. A financial institution can operate only through financial investment or manipulation, and these, as it is hoped to make clear, are in themselves the fundamental cause of the world's difficulties.

CHAPTER IV

THE GAP BETWEEN PRICES AND PURCHASING POWER

IT may reasonably be asked why a system which, on the face of it, does not appear to have undergone important modifications during the past hundred years or so, has become so powerful and so oppressive. A correct answer to this question is probably of more importance than the solution of any other problem before the world at the present time.

A student of the preceding pages will have grasped the important fact that money is not made by industry. Neither is it made by agriculture, or by any manufacturing progress. The farmer who grows a ton of potatoes does not grow the money whereby the ton of potatoes may be bought, and if he is fortunate enough to sell them, he merely gets money which someone else had previously.

27

Purchasing power, therefore, is not, as might be gathered from the current discussions on the subject, an emanation from the production of real commodities or services much like the scent from a rose, but on the contrary, is produced by an entirely distinct process, that is to say, the banking system. Bearing this in mind, we can understand that it is impossible for a closed community to operate continuously on the profit system, if the amount of money inside this community is not increased, *even though the amount of goods and services available are not increased*. This obvious but commonly overlooked fact forms the justification, if any, for the idea on which Socialist policy for the past hundred years has been based—that the poor are poor because the rich are rich. If a number of persons continue to sell articles at a greater price than that paid for them, they must eventually come into possession of all the money in the community, and the only flaw in such a state of affairs would be that it would be self-destructive, since in a comparatively short period of time a small section of the

28

community would own all the money, and therefore the remainder of the community would be unable to pay, and production and sale would stop. This process probably contributed largely to the rapid accumulation of wealth in the hands of the *entrepreneur* at the beginning of the nineteenth century, and the limited extent to which the benefits of industrial progress were passed on to the general population; but the profit-making system is certainly not to any great extent responsible for the present situation, since profits have ceased to form an outstanding feature of business. It is an extraordinary feature of the controversy that they are attacked as immoral as well as undesirable. It has never been clear to me why any man in any position of life should be expected to perform any action whatever which was not in *some* sense of the word profitable to him, and there is more than a suspicion that the attack upon profits can ultimately be traced to a fear of the economic security offered by this type of remuneration, as compared with that of the wage and salary.

29

The factor which is probably at the root of the problem is at once more complex and more subtle, and has during the past few years been a matter of acrimonious controversy. On its physical or realistic side it is intimately connected with the replacement of human labour by machine labour.

The physical effects of this replacement are not difficult to apprehend. If one unit of human labour with the aid of mechanical power and machinery will produce ten times as much as the same unit working without such aids, it is obvious that there will either be ten times as much production or only one-tenth the amount of labour will be required.

The productivity of a unit of human labour has increased somewhat irregularly over the whole field of production. In some cases the increase in a hundred years has amounted to thousands per cent, in some cases the increase of output per unit has been much less. It is, however, broadly true to say that general economic production, which may be defined as the conversion of existing materials into a form suitable for human use, is proportional to the rate at which energy of any description is used in the process, and this line of attack is probably closer to reality than any method in which financial units are employed.

On this basis it is safe to say that one unit of human labour can on the average produce at least forty times as much as was the case up to the beginning of the nineteenth century. The following examples are some indication of the progress made in the past few years alone.

The rate of production of pig-iron is three times as great per man employed as it was in 1914. A workman using automatic machines can make 4,000 glass bottles as quickly as he could have made 100 by hand twenty-five years ago. In 1919 the index of factory output (based upon 1914 as 100) was 146, and the index of factory employment was 129. By 1927 output had risen to 170, but employment had sunk to 115. In 1928 American farmers were using 45,000 harvesting and threshing machines, and with

31

them had displaced 130,000 farm hands. In automobiles, output per man has increased to 310 per cent, an increase of 210 per cent.

When we approach the question of distribution, however, we find a remarkable discrepancy. Professor Paul H. Douglas states in his examination of the problem that, in the first quarter of the twentieth century, real wages increased 30 per cent, productivity per employee increased by 54 per cent. In 1923 production increased 38 per cent, but consumption by wage-earners 32 per cent. In 1925 production increased 54 per cent, but consumption only 30 per cent. These latter figures compare with 1913 as a basis.

Eliminating the pseudo-moral complications commonly introduced into this aspect of the subject, it is clear that certain consequences were bound to ensue. Either the requirements of the population must increase at the rate at which the capacity for production increases, and at the same time the financial mechanism must be adjusted to provide for the distribution of the production, or a decreasing number of persons would be required in production. Unless the wages of this decreasing number of individuals collectively rises to the amount which, previously distributed to a larger number of workers, would buy the still greater production, either costs and prices must fall, or an increasing proportion of the goods must be unsold to the persons who produced them. Certain consequences, readily understood if it be remembered that wages, costs, and purchasing power are only different aspects of the same thing, accompany a continuous fall in *costs* under the existing financial system, and a fall of *prices*, while off-setting these consequences to some extent, involves the *entrepreneur* in a loss on the whole of his stocks, a loss which he is not usually willing, or indeed able, to take.

The first aspect of this complex situation which demands attention is the financing of capital production by means of the reinvestment of savings, which, it should be noticed, is the method commonly stated to be the proper method. It is doubtful whether more than an insignificant proportion of financing is done in this way, the greater part coming from new credits supplied by banks and insurance companies in return for debentures, but it forms the smoke-screen which conceals the fact that public issues are in the main acquired by financial institutions through the medium of drafts upon themselves. The growth of insurance has no doubt been a considerable factor in accelerating the process. If we consider the case of a workman earning, let us say, £5 per week, who saves £1 of this and at the end of a hundred weeks subscribes for shares in a new manufacturing company, the effect is not hard to trace. The original £5 per week was wages paid to the workman, and these wages were, by the orthodox costing system, debited to the cost of the articles produced by his employer. Eventually, due to his saving, these articles cannot be sold, as a simple arithmetical proposition shows, since he has taken 20 per cent of the necessary purchasing power off the market. His investment of this 20 per cent we may assume results in the manufacture of machinery in which his £100 again appears as wages. Assuming that no physical deterioration has taken place, or that the goods have not been exported, the 20 per cent deficiency in the first cycle of production has now been restored, and the original goods could be bought. But the machinery which has been made in the second cycle of production is now a charge on further production for which no purchasing power whatever exists. This proposition may be generalised as follows : *Where any payment in money appears twice or more in series production, then the ultimate price of the product is increased by the amount of that payment multiplied by the number of times of its appearance, without any equivalent increase of purchasing power.*

With this fundamental proposition in mind we are in a position to take a more generalised view of the defect in the price system which is concerned with the double circuit of money in industry, and which has become known as the A plus B theorem. The statement of this is as follows: In any manufacturing undertaking the payments made may be divided into two groups: Group A: Payments made to individuals as wages, salaries, and dividends; Group B: Payments made to other organisations for raw materials, bank charges, and other external costs. The rate of distribution of purchasing power to individuals is represented by A, but since all payments go into prices, the rate of generation of prices cannot be less than A plus B. Since A will not purchase A plus B, a proportion of the product at least equivalent to B must be distributed by a form of purchasing power which is not comprised in the description grouped under A.

Now the first objection which is commonly raised to this statement is that the payments in wages which are made to the public for intermediate products which the public does not want to buy and could not use, when added together, make up the necessary sum to balance the B payments, so that the population can buy all the consumable products. But an examination of the diagram on page 37 will show that this is not a satisfactory explanation. If we imagine

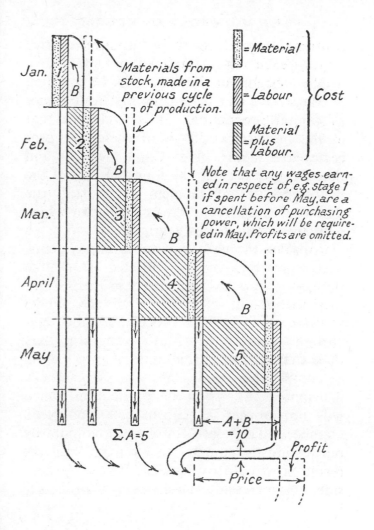

consumable products to be produced in five stages, each stage taking one month, a product begun in January will be finished in May. We can regard the first four stages as capital production. It is irrelevant that in the modern world all of these five processes are taking place simultaneously and that the product may be found in any of the five stages at any moment. It is still true that you cannot bake bread with corn which you are simultaneously grinding.

Consider the nature of these B payments. They are repayments collected from the public of purchasing power in respect of production not yet delivered to the public. If the wage-earners in process "I" use their current month's, i.e. May's, wages to buy their share of one current month's production of consumable goods, they are using money distributed in respect of production which will not appear as consumable goods till October. They are in fact involuntarily reinvesting their money in industry, with the result previously explained. When we consider the increasing sub-division of process—

and in "process" we may include the using of machine-tools, buildings, and the general plant of the country—it will readily be understood that this period shown as five months in the diagram may easily cover many years.

As the economic system may be said to depend upon this matter, it is essential that a clear understanding of it should be obtained.

Let us imagine a capitalist to own a certain piece of land, on which is a house, and a building containing the necessary machinery for preparing, spinning, and weaving linen, and that the land is capable of growing in addition to flax, all the food necessary to maintain a man. Let us further imagine that the capitalist in the first place allows a man to live free of all payment in the house and to have the use of all the foodstuffs that he grows on condition that he also grows, spins, and weaves a certain amount of linen for the capitalist. Let us further imagine that after a time this arrangement is altered by the payment to the man of £1 a week for the work on the linen business, but that this £1 is taken back each week as rent for the house and payment for the foodstuffs.

Let us now imagine that from the time the flax is picked to the time that the linen is delivered to the capitalist, a period of six weeks elapses. Obviously the cost of the linen must be £6, and this will be the price, plus profit, which the capitalist would place upon it. Quite obviously only one-sixth of the purchasing power necessary to buy the linen is now available, although " at some time or other" all the £6 has been distributed. It should also be noticed that the arrangement is a perfectly equitable arrangement. The employee obtains definite return for his services in the form of bed, board, and clothes, which quite probably he might not have been able to obtain had not the knowledge and organisation of the capitalist brought together housing, flax, food, and machinery. In other words, the problem disclosed is not a moral problem, it is an arithmetical problem.

Let us now imagine that half of the employee's time is devoted to making a machine which will do all the work of preparing and manufacturing linen, and that the manufacture of this machine takes twelve weeks. We may therefore say that the machine costs £6, the total value of the production of machine and flax being still £1 per week. At the end of this period the machine is substituted for the man, the machine being driven, we suppose, by the burning of the food which was previously consumed by the man, and the machine being housed in the house previously occupied by the man, and being automatic. The capitalist will be justified in saying that the cost of the operation of the machine is £1 per week as before, and if there is any wear, he will also be justified in allocating the cost of this wear to the cost of the linen. It should be noticed, however, that he will now not distribute any money at all, since it is obviously no use offering a £1 note a week to a machine. He will merely allocate this cost, and once again the allocation will be perfectly fair and proper, but no one will be able to pay the price, because no one has received any money.

In the modern industrial system, this process can be identified easily in the form of

41

machine charges. For instance, a modern stamping plant may require to add 600 per cent to its labour charges to cover its machine charges, this sum not being in any true sense profit. In such a case, for every £1 expended in a given period in wages, £6, making £7 in all, would be carried forward into prices. Although this is an extreme case, the constant, and in one sense desirable, tendency is for direct charges to decrease and for indirect charges to increase as a result of the replacement of human labour by machinery. There is no difference between a plant charge of this nature and a similar sum repaid as a "B" payment. The essential point is that when a given sum of money leaves the consumer on its journey back to the point of origin in the bank it is on its way to extinction. If that extinction takes place before the extinction of the price value created during its journey *from* the bank, then each such operation produces a corresponding disequilibrium between money and prices. For these causes and others of a similar character, it seems to me quite beyond argument that

42

the production of such a quantity of intermediate products, including plant, machinery, buildings, and so forth, as is physically necessary to maintain a given quantity of consumable products, will not provide a distribution of purchasing power sufficient to buy these consumable products. This would be true even if prices and costs were identical. But since prices can and do rise much above costs, additional purchasing power from intermediate production is rapidly absorbed.

To say that at some time or other the money has been distributed is in the nature of a general assertion which does not bear upon the specific fact. The mill will never grind with the water that has passed, and unless it can be shown, as it certainly cannot be shown, that all these sums distributed in respect of the production of intermediate products are actually saved up, not in the form of securities, but in the form of actual purchasing power, we are obliged to assume what I believe to be true, that the rate of flow of purchasing power derived from the normal and theoretical operation of the existing price system is always less than that of the generation of prices within the same period of time.

There is another method of regarding this matter which is helpful to the grasp of an admittedly difficult subject. Suppose that the wages, salaries, and dividends distributed *were* exactly sufficient to buy the new production on sale at any moment and did so buy it, i.e. let us suppose that the financial system worked as it is supposed to work. Obviously numbers of things would be bought, such as houses, furniture, etc., which would have a considerable life. But *ex hypothesi* the sale *between consumers* (as distinguished from sales from producer to consumer) of these would be impossible—they would have no money, since at the moment of transfer of the goods from the producing to the consuming system their money value would have disappeared on its journey back to the bank, to finance a fresh cycle of production.

Sales between *consumers* are an important though frequently overlooked factor in distribution, and require that the *money value*

44

of " second-hand " goods shall be in existence until the goods have physically disappeared.

It may, with reason, be asked how if this be so, is it that in fact consumable products are sold at all? The answer to this is again complex, but the main forms in which assistance is given to the defective purchasing power of the population (although that assistance is much less than is required to enable the production system fully to be drawn upon) are the redistribution of money through the social services such as the so-called dole, the use of money received from the sale of exports, from foreign investments and from invisible exports such as shipping, redistributed through the medium of taxation, the distribution of bank loans (advanced on mortgage, debentures, etc.) in wages for excessive capital production, and the selling of goods below cost through the agency of bankruptcies, forced sales, and actual destruction. These latter three are a direct discouragement to production, and in fact represent a subsidy in aid of prices from private sources, a conception which it is

45

desirable to bear in mind in considering remedies, in view of the fact that, so far from this subsidy raising prices, it comes into operation only by the lowering of prices.

It is also clear that the longer the average period over which money is collected in respect of the creation and destruction of a capital asset (which corresponds to the "life" of an asset), and the shorter the average period over which money is collected for day-to-day living on the part of the community (which corresponds to the "life" of consumable goods), the greater will be the discrepancy between purchasing power and prices.

The former period is the average time in years (N_2) taken to make and wear out a capital asset; it is the time covered by the production and destruction of a cost. Obviously, such a period will vary greatly according to the nature of the asset, but a fair and usual average is twenty years.

The latter period is the average time in years (N_1) during which the money at the disposal of the community (total income) circulates from industry to the consumer and back again.

"In Great Britain, for instance, the deposits in the Joint Stock Banks are roughly £2,000,000,000. In rough figures, the annual clearings of the clearing banks amount to £40,000,000,000. It seems obvious that the £2,000,000,000 of deposits must circulate twenty times in a year to produce these clearing-house figures, and that therefore the average rate of circulation is a little over two and a half weeks. . . . The clearing-house figures just quoted contain a large number of 'butcher-baker' (second-hand) transactions, and these must be deducted in estimating circulation rates."[1]

After making the necessary correction for the volume of second-hand transactions and for payments that do not go through the clearing-house, we may conclude that the average period of circulation of the money spent upon consumable goods is about two months, or one-sixth of one year.

[1] C. H. Douglas, "The New and the Old Economics," pp.18, 19

The effect of the very great disparity between these two rates is as follows :

Let $n_1 = \dfrac{1}{N_1}$ = number of circulations per year, say 6.

Let $n_2 = \dfrac{1}{N_2}$ = number of circulations per year, say $\dfrac{1}{20}$.

Let A = all disbursements by a manufacturer which create costs

= wages and salaries.

Let B = all disbursements by a manufacturer which transfer costs

= payments to other organisations.

The manufacturer pays £A per annum into the N_1 system, and £B per annum into the N_2 system.

Disregarding profit, the price of production is £$(A + B)$ per annum. But to purchase (i.e. to cancel the allocated cost of £$(A + B)$) there is present in the hands of the consumer :—

48

$$\frac{\pounds(An_1 + Bn_2)}{n_1} = \pounds\left(A + B\frac{n_2}{n_1}\right)$$

Consequently, the rate of production of price values exceeds the rate at which they can be cancelled by the purchasing power in the hands of the consumer by an amount proportional to

$$B\left(1 - \frac{n_2}{n_1}\right) = \text{approximately } B.$$

This deficit may be made up by the export of goods on credit, by the writing down of goods below cost, by bankruptcies, and by money distributed for public works and charged to debt. But in the main it is represented by mounting debt.

It will readily be seen how this situation in which, not production, but money, is chronically insufficient, must transfer control to the institutions which have acquired the monopoly of money-making. In order that the industrial system may not grind to a standstill, an increasing issue of money, chiefly for capital production, is necessary

49

to bridge the gap between purchasing power and prices—a gap which is the only possible explanation of the anomaly between a half-idle production system and a half-starving population. But as this fresh money is claimed by the banking system, and has to be repaid, the situation is cumulatively worsened.

While the question of War Debts is in essence only a special, if important, case of the generalised statement, it does in fact lend itself to a conclusive demonstration of the defective accounting system we call Finance. Any realist will appreciate that a war is paid for (physically) as it is fought. The material, the guns, shells, aeroplanes, are the result of work done and matter converted, and when used they are destroyed. Clearly an accounting system which implies (*a*) that an asset exists corresponding to the securities held in the form of War Bonds, and (*b*) that there is any physical process going on corresponding to "taxing the country to pay for the War," must obviously be fallacious. If the taxes were applied to making exactly

50

the same amount of material destroyed in the War, then the public would have both the war material and the taxes, in the form of saved wages.

CHAPTER V

THE MEANING OF A BALANCED BUDGET

WE are now in a position to examine a fundamental axiom of national finance as at present conducted, which is that budgets must be balanced, by which is meant that all Governmental expenditure must normally be recovered from the individuals in the country by means of taxation.

Now like so many other of the axioms of finance, this proposition seems on the face of it to be incontrovertible. We are all familiar with Charles Dickens's exemplification of it: "Income £20, expenditure £19 19s. 6d., result, happiness. Income £20, expenditure £20 0s. 6d., result, misery." So valuable a piece of financial propaganda, incidentally, is sufficient to have facilitated the success of that author even were it otherwise undeserved.

In the case of the individual, to spend more than you receive is a policy which cannot be

53

pursued with success for any length of time. But when we come to examine the proposition as applied to a nation, in the light of the analysis of the financial system in the foregoing chapters, we find that the cases are not in any sense parallel. In the case of the individual, income is purchasing power which is received from some other source, either for services rendered or for securities held. We are already aware that this purchasing power proceeds from the banks in the form of loans, and has to be repaid to the banks. Therefore it is perfectly true to say that the income of the individual is money which has been issued by the banks on loan and is merely held by the individual on its way back to the banks for a greater or less time according to the rate at which banks are calling in their outstanding loans.

Bearing this in mind, let us consider the meaning of taxation, and for the moment it will be sufficient to consider what is called direct taxation, that is to say, taxation of profit and incomes as distinct from indirect taxation in the form of duty on specific products.

Let us suppose that a manufacturing firm, Messrs. Brown & Co., draws £1,000 from a bank with which to pay wages and salaries, which, for the sake of argument, are all subject to income tax. It is at the moment irrelevant whether this £1,000 does or does not constitute an overdraft. Leaving out of consideration overhead charges this £1,000 produces *prices* of £1,000 plus Messrs. Brown's profit which we will say is 10 per cent, or a total of £1,100. This £1,100 has to be collected from the public in prices.

Now in the first place the Government collects from Messrs. Brown, let us say 4*s*. in the £ on £100 profit, or £20. If we assume Messrs. Brown to employ ten individuals, each receiving £100, £20 will be subtracted from each of them, making a total of £220. Each of these ten individuals, who, we will assume, shop exclusively at a departmental store which supplies everything they require, will spend, let us say, £50 in buying goods which cost the departmental store £40. The £10 per person is the profit of the departmental store amounting to £100. Of this profit the

Government again takes in taxation £20. making £240. The departmental store pays £10 of the £50 which it receives per person to its own employees as wages, amounting to a further £100. Of this the Government again takes £20 (since this is the income of the employees), making £260. Or to put the matter shortly, every time money passes from one set of hands to another, what is expenditure in the first set of hands becomes income for the second set of hands, and at each transfer it is taxed at, let us say, 20 per cent. Mathematically, the whole of the money will be taken in taxation if it passes through an infinite number of hands. So that ultimately the individuals comprising the nation would have two creditors, each of whom would have a claim on the whole of the purchasing power distributed: firstly, Messrs. Brown, for goods supplied, and secondly, the nation, which in the mathematical limit would collect the whole of it in taxation no matter what the rate of taxation might be. If it be argued that the State had already distributed this sum in wages for national services, then, of course, the reply is that if all the wages and salaries distributed by the Government are taken back in taxation, all Government products should be distributed free and the National Debt cancelled.

But in fact it is quite easy to ascertain that the individual national has ultimately only one creditor who, apart from interest, doubles every loan made by him. The great spending departments, such as the War Office, the Admiralty, the Office of Works, and others, obtain the money with which to make their monthly payments by means of drafts upon what is called the "Ways and Means Account," which is in fact merely a Governmental overdraft kept with the Bank of England. The Bank of England treats this overdraft of the Government as cash which, since it rests upon the credit of the country, it is clearly entitled to do. The sums received in taxation go to the Reduction of the Government debit on the Ways and Means Account, so that we have the position that the money which the Government spends is created by the Bank of England, is loaned to the Government, and is

57

repaid by taxation of wages, salaries and dividends, which were originally derived from this and other bank loans, which, in turn, have to be repaid[1].

The impossibility of a balanced budget within a closed system of credit must be from the foregoing sufficiently obvious. Without going into details which still further complicate the situation, such a proposition means that the only surplus purchasing power at the disposal of the individuals comprising the nation would be the excess of bank loans over bank repayments, i.e. debt, together with the excess of money received for exports over money payments for imports, which is, of course, the explanation of the statement commonly made that Great Britain lives upon its exports. It is an extraordinary instance of the confusion of mind which has been produced by interested propaganda.

It will be clear that the demand for a balanced budget is another form of the claim that all money belongs to the banks, and so

[1]Complete repayment would mean that the recipients of State wages and salaries would, in a nationalised State, pay taxes equal to 20s. in the £ and have no purchasing power.

far from being a reflection of the physical facts of production, is unrelated to them. Every modern community, so far as physical facts are concerned, is becoming richer year by year, and this increase of riches could be greatly accelerated, a fact which is indicated by a large unemployed population, and a manufacturing system with a capacity which, although already greatly in excess of present possibilities of sale, is daily being improved. It is equally obvious that so long as this demand for a balanced national budget is admitted, there can be no economic security, since it involves continuous application to the financial authorities for permission to live.

CHAPTER VI

THE GOLD STANDARD AND BANKING POLICY

IT will be evident from the examination of the organisation of the price and credit issue system, that the price system as understood by the producer, and the price system as assumed, and in fact operated, by the banking system, are not the same system. The producer carries on business on the assumption that he will be able to add together the whole of his costs, that is to say, disbursements, in one form or another, not merely of wages, but of charges which he must recover in respect of his capital outlay, and put this accumulated cost, plus his own variable remuneration in the form of profit, on to the public. Obviously his ability to do this depends both on the possession by the public of sufficient purchasing power to meet these charges and the psychological wish to acquire the goods which the producer places at its disposal.

61

But in Chapter III we have seen that ultimately the amount of money in the community depends not on the action of producers, but on the policy of the banking system, and leaving aside for the moment all questions of high politics, the banker, being essentially a dealer in a commodity called money, is fundamentally concerned to make that commodity as valuable as possible. He is normally a deflationist, since low prices mean a high value for the monetary unit, and facilitate not only the internal business of the banks, but their foreign exchange operations which are regarded by them as of greater importance. The producer, therefore, is caught between an inflexible cost system which in Great Britain is rendered particularly rigid by trades union regulations in regard to wage rates and conditions, and a price system which is based on a chronic scarcity of money arising from two sources, the first purely mathematical, and the second a matter of policy.

It is obvious that such a state of affairs, cumulative because of the increasing gravity of the mathematical defect involved in the costing of machine production, places the banking system in complete control of the economic system. Before examining the use which has been made of this commanding position, it is perhaps desirable to consider recent developments in banking organisation and their apparent objective.

The fundamental proposition of the modern banking system is that the basis of credit is currency.

So far as the subject is becoming a matter for public controversy, it would be easy to imagine that the point at issue was largely, if not entirely, a question of the merits or demerits of a pure or modified Gold Standard currency system. But in fact, as I trust has emerged from the matter covered by the previous pages, this is not the fundamental problem which arises from the essential nature of money as defined as effective demand. It is not now seriously questioned by any responsible authority, orthodox or otherwise, that the major portion of this effective demand is actually and literally created by the banking system, and is claimed as its property. This amounts to the same thing as claiming (although not necessarily exercising) the ownership of all goods and services, and is, in fact, a return by an ingenious route to the claim that all property, persons, and things, belong to the King, substituting, however, in this case, the financial system for the King. From the standpoint of ethics the position seems untenable, since the contribution towards the general welfare made by the financial system as compared, let us say, with that made by scientists, engineers, and organisers, would appear to be negligible. And from the pragmatic point of view with which modern ideas are more in sympathy, the claim seems to be still more difficult to sustain. The social unrest, international friction, and the largely unsatisfactory nature of modern civilisation, can be directly traced to it. A system which will not allow the population of the world to obtain goods which are already in existence, without first obtaining money through the making of further goods which are not, and may never be, required, is the direct explanation of the senseless strain and hurry of the modern business world.

But so far as banking is concerned, there is little doubt that the Gold Standard, so called, is a factor in the policy which it is intended to pursue, and for this reason, if for no other, some examination of it seems desirable.

The difficulty in dealing with the subject arises largely from the fact that it has never at any time been what it pretends to be. Originally gold itself was supposed to represent the only true and universally accepted claim for goods. Previously to 1914 the gold sovereign circulated freely in Great Britain, and the illusion of a gold currency was fairly successful. Within two days of the outbreak of war in 1914, however, the available stocks of gold sovereigns had been withdrawn from the banks by depositors who imagined that in this way they were safeguarding their possessions, with a result that it was necessary to declare a moratorium, during the progress of which, treasury notes of a face value of £1 and 10s. were printed in large numbers and handed over to the banks for issue to their depositors. The fact that the Gold Standard was a fraudulent standard was demonstrated in twenty-four hours.

The smoothness of the transition from the issue of the gold sovereign to that of the paper £ surprised even the bankers who were most concerned. It may be remarked in passing that one of the major tragedies of the War, not less fruitful in human distress and as far-reaching in its results as the War itself, took place when the representatives of the Government[1] acceded to the demands of the bankers that the treasury note should be issued only through the banks and should be handed over in return for advances of bank credit. The effect of this was, in the first place, to place the credit of sectional and private institutions, such as the banks, higher than that of the Government itself, and still further to intensify the control of finance upon business in general.

During the years 1914-1918, however, this control was not much felt. " *Inter arma silent*

---

[1] " He did everything we asked of him."—Sir Edward Holden of Mr. Lloyd George.

leges." The banks and other financial institutions were during that period put in their proper place as agents for the execution of the expressed policy of the country at large, and no question of money was allowed to enter into the desirability of physical action. It need hardly be said, nor is it, I think, astonishing, that the conduct of this financial policy was not free from glaring technical mistakes. It did, however, serve to demonstrate beyond peradventure that the idea that a physical policy cannot be carried out unless there is, as the phrase goes, sufficient money with which to do it is, as it has always been, an illusion fostered for interested purposes.

On the onslaught of peace, however, the financial authorities realised that it was imperative, from their point of view, to regain control of the situation. After the lapse of a short period of feverish production and industrial prosperity, accompanied by rapidly rising prices, the policy of deflation was simultaneously inaugurated in the United States and Great Britain about April, 1920. The effects were immediate. In the United

States the numbers of unemployed rose from negligible figures to six millions within three months, and in Great Britain effects proportionate to the size of the population were similarly experienced. In the United States this policy was reversed after a period of about six months, to be followed by eight years of the greatest material prosperity ever experienced by any country in history, during which the deposits in the Member Banks of the Federal Reserve System rose by £1,873,000,000. For reasons which appear to be connected with the subservience of the Bank of England to the Federal Reserve Bank of the U.S.A., the policy of deflation was pursued in Great Britain, almost alone amongst industrial countries, with results which are fresh in the memory, but which may be conveniently visualised upon examination of the chart on page 135. During this period the deposits in the five large joint stock banks together rose by only £16,000,000.

The policy of deflation in Great Britain was divided into two stages, the first stage consisting in a rapid reduction in the total amount of currency notes in circulation, the figure being in the first place fixed at £348 millions as a result of provision that the total in any year should not exceed the minimum circulation of the preceding year. Since the stagnation of trade was itself a prime cause in the reduction of the circulation of treasury notes, a progressive reduction from year to year was inevitable, and by 1928 the total of Bank of England and treasury notes had fallen to £260,000,000. The Federal Reserve Bulletin, in contrast, remarked in December, 1926, that the volume of money in circulation in the U.S.A. on November 1st was larger by £32,000,000 than at the corresponding date in 1925.

The legal liability of the joint stock banks being to deliver legal tender upon demand in the case of their current accounts, and after an agreed period in the case of time deposits, the automatic result of the reduction of treasury notes was to reduce by probably ten times the amount of this reduction the amount of credit which the banks were prepared to extend to industry. The effect was that which might logically be expected: the amount distributed in wages in the country fell, although the wage rates to a large extent did not. The purchasing power of the country was diminished, and stocks were thrown upon the market at heavy losses to the producers, with the desired effect that prices fell, not because cost of production fell, but because the producer provided from his own resources a subsidy in aid of cost by selling at a loss. In 1925 the process was accelerated by the restoration of a modified Gold Standard, and in 1928 the Government handed over the note issue to the Bank of England.

The theory of the Gold Standard £ is that it represents 113 grains of fine gold, or conversely that gold will always be bought by the Bank of England at 84s. an ounce. Since, e.g. a United States dollar represented a fixed quantity of gold (about 23 grains) the value of one gold currency in terms of another is assumed to be approximately stable. To prevent the possibility of gold being acquired to any extent by other than financial institutions, the statute by which Great Britain was restored to a gold basis of currency enacted that not less than a standard gold bar worth about £1,700 would be delivered on demand. In order that the exchange may theoretically indicate the balance of trade, the limits at which a central bank must buy or sell gold are laid down. "Standard" gold (eleven-twelfths fine) has a minimum and maximum price of £3 17s. 9d. and £3 17s. 10½d. respectively. The actual point at which it pays to buy gold for shipment obviously varies with shipment rates, insurance, and interest.

In 1933 the United States repudiated its liability to redeem its gold certificates, and in 1936 the "gold content" of the dollar is about 13 grains.

It will be understood that if the Gold Standard or rather the Gold Exchange Standard worked automatically and were universal, it would simply amount to the establishment of a common unit of currency, irrespective of international boundaries, with gold as the "interpreter" through which all interchange of currency would have to pass. But a little reflection will show that such a condition cannot in fact exist under the actual economic and political conditions which are parallel to it. In the first place, the available amount of gold bears no ratio to anything in particular. Currency in itself, whether linked by a Gold Standard or otherwise, is meaningless except in relation to the goods and services which it will command. Both goods and services are themselves priced by units of currency ultimately depending, not upon how much gold they will buy, but upon how much goods and services they will command *at the place at which the goods and services are required.* Since wage rates, salaries, and conventional remunerations are more or less rigidly fixed, the *cost* of production is not affected so much by the amount of money available as by these conventional wage and salary rates, so that while a Gold Standard or in fact *any* currency basis of credit *may* secure interchangeability between the currency of one country and another country, it cannot in any way guarantee that the interchangeable unit of currency will buy the same amount of goods. There are, of course, other complicating factors,

72

such as tariffs, which still further accentuate the essential element of locality, and the hostility to measures of this description has arisen in the main from financial interests, desirous of remaining the sole arbiters of trade.

Owing to the immense pyramid of purchasing power inverted on a small gold base, exports of gold produce money stringency of a violent character out of all proportion to the amount exported, and bearing no relation either to productive capacity or physical demand.

The vicissitudes of the Gold Standard in Great Britain are a matter of common knowledge, but certain aspects of it can be grasped conveniently from the curves on page 135.

Since for every seller there must be a buyer, the situation which was created by the numerous and increasing number of bankruptcies and forced sales merits some attention. The momentum of business induces business undertakings to carry on to a point considerably beyond that justified by their unmortgaged liquid resources, even assuming that their transactions have been financed normally in this way. As a result of this, and as indeed might be expected from the control over the money system acquired by the banking institutions, it is probably true to say that in Great Britain, 90 per cent of trade and business has come into the possession or control of banking interests. Such a tremendous transfer of ownership has probably never occurred in recorded history.

The banker *per se* has not, in general, technical knowledge outside the routine of banking. On two notable occasions the heads of large banking institutions, one in Canada (Sir Frederick Williams-Taylor of the Bank of Montreal) and the other in England (Mr. Montagu Norman of the Bank of England) have replied to questions regarding the results to be expected from current banking policy in almost identical terms, to the effect that they were bankers, not economists, a contention which, viewed in the light of events, seems to be true. It is not to be wondered at, therefore, on the principle that there is nothing like leather, that the

74

bankers' immediate reaction to the day-by-day acquisition of large businesses has been to put them under the control of chartered accountants, with the result that a financial result rather than a physical result has been aimed at. Plant has been broken up, since its operation could not be justified by the profits to be expected in existing circumstances (even though its physical product was urgently required), buildings, with the exception of those erected for the use of financial institutions, have been cut down both in quality and design with disastrous results to the amenities of the country at large, agricultural properties have deteriorated, and technical enterprise has been stifled. A further complication is introduced as a result of the predominant holding of National Debt securities by banks and insurance companies, resulting in the chartered accountant, acting for them, being often a scarcely veiled tax-collector.

There have been many critics of this policy, not alone amongst specialists on the question of monetary science, but in the ranks of both industry and banking itself. Parliamentary discussion, industrial protests, and technical criticism, however, have been alike without any apparent influence upon the policy pursued, which in the main has not even been defended. The effect of such criticism, if any, must be sought in the acceleration of the measures taken to increase the strength of bank organisation against this and similar attacks, a major feature being the formation of twenty-eight central banks in the past decade, culminating in the launching of the super-central bank known as the Bank of International Settlements.

This institution opened its doors in May, 1930, ostensibly to deal with the transfer of the large sums of money involved in the International Debts and reparations, which are the legacy of the Peace Treaties. As frequently happens in connection with financial affairs, the ostensible objective of the bank, however, can be recognised as a cover for much larger activities.

The constitution of the bank can be understood by examination of the disposition of its capital, the separation of this capital from voting rights, and the composition of its Board of Directors. It is incorporated under a charter from the Swiss Government, protected by a convention between Switzerland and the Governments principally interested in reparations, which are also, of course, the Governments forming the titular representatives of the major financial interests. Situated in Basle, it is geographically protected from physical or military pressure which would not at the same time involve a violation of Swiss neutrality. It may be noticed that this extraterritoriality, which is, in the case of the Bank of International Settlements, achieved by actual geographical means, is in the case of the smaller central banks previously referred to as having come into existence since the War, claimed as a legal right in their constitutions. Since the shares do not carry any voting rights, and since a bank of this description could obviously, if necessary, dispense with any financial capital, the shareholding is not a matter of any special interest. The constitution of the Board of Directors, however, is a different matter. It consists, first, of the governors of the central banks of Belgium, France, Germany, Great Britain, and Italy, with a nominee of the Bank of Japan, and a representative of United States banking. Added to this are seven additional directors nominated individually by the first seven, having the same nationalities as their nominators, and "representative of finance, industry, or commerce". The central banks of France and Germany have the further power, during the period of the reparation payments, to appoint one more member each, which they have done. There being a maximum of only nine other seats on the Board, it is clear that the original central banks constituting the appointers of the first directors have permanent control over the policies of the bank. This control is further emphasised by a provision that voting rights at general meetings are in proportion to the number of shares *originally* allotted to those institutions having the power of nomination to the Board.

While the United States of America would not at first sight appear to be primarily interested, the peculiar position of the Bank of

England, whose Governor would appear to be largely the representative of American financial policy, should be noted, as well as the fact that the first President, Mr. Gates McGarrah, is an American closely connected with large American financial interests.

The objects of the Bank are defined in its statutes as being "to promote the co-operation of central banks and to provide additional facilities for international financial operations, and to act as trustee or agent in regard to international financial settlements entrusted to it under agreements with the parties concerned." Obviously the intention of this was that the B.I.S. should be essentially the Central Bank of central banks, that it should hold reserves of gold as a basis of the cash reserves of the central banks, and that in consequence it should act as the supreme regulator of the world's money supplies. In other words, for instance, the relation of the Bank of England to the B.I.S. would be similar to that of the joint stock banks to the Bank of England, and thus it may be said that the B.I.S. places the final stone upon the pyramid

79

of financial organisation.

There is a sufficiently comprehensive literature upon the organisation and technique of the banking system to make it unnecessary to deal with the matter in detail. The objective of the preceding examination of the constitution of the B.I.S., which may be regarded as the final development of the system, is to afford material by which the general policy of the banking system may be recognised.

While no doubt the working banker would be tempted to deny it, it seems true beyond all reasonable doubt to say that the system is directed to the constitution of a series of bottle-necks in the organisation of the economic system, these bottle-necks operating through the financial system to place both production and distribution under the control of financial interests. In the modern world, the considerable sums of purchasing power which are required to finance industrial undertakings cannot be obtained without access to the mechanism of public credit which has come under the control of this system. The joint stock banks, therefore, may be said to be in control at this point. Their own adherence to the system in Great Britain is insured by their dependency upon the Bank of England for currency, and in other countries by somewhat similar arrangements in regard to the central banks. These central banks in turn are, by the costing system, forced to make provision for considerable transactions in the various national currencies, and these transactions as between nations are destined to come under the control of the Bank of International Settlements, which obviously places the power of veto on the interchange of industrial commodities, as between nations, with this latter institution. It is a marvellous system, and it would be a gross admission of irresponsibility to condemn it without the most careful examination.

CHAPTER VII

THE RESULTS OF BANKING CONTROL

PERHAPS the major difficulty which confronts the student of large-scale organisation is to decide to what extent it is practicable to question principles which have been regarded as axiomatic. While there has been continuous conflict of opinion in regard to forms of government, the necessity for government of some kind has not in responsible quarters seriously been questioned. Yet on the face of it, government, in the sense in which it is commonly understood, can easily be put upon its defence, and has in fact throughout history been continuously upon its defence. There is essentially no difference between the principles of modern government and those of the most oppressive of the tyrannies of history. The mechanism is different, the results on the whole may be considerably more satisfactory, but in each case the essential consists in an infringement upon personal liberty.

It would be anachronistic to inject into the consideration of this situation any question of what are called human rights. Perhaps the clearest fact which emerges from the present flux in the world of ideas and of action is that the human individual has no rights except those which he can sustain. It does not, however, seem to require much consideration to admit that the general interest is well served by the elimination of certain courses of action on the part of the individual, murder being perhaps an instance. But having arrived at this point, we have by no means disposed of the fundamental problem. What is it which causes murder, and do we deal most satisfactorily with the problem of murder by the imposition of severe penalties upon the murderer, or on the other hand by concentrating the whole forces of society to remove any incentive to murder? Or, to put the matter another way, is murder a form of mental aberration, or is it a reaction from an environment which can be changed?

84

As a practical problem there is probably no clear answer to this dilemma in the present stage of human progress. It is arguable that we could eliminate murder if we could with sufficient rapidity modify the predisposing causes to murder which are involved in a defective economic and social system, and at the same time remove the mental complexes which have been produced by those defects. But it cannot be done by a stroke of the pen, or by any action, governmental or otherwise, which is in the range of practical politics ; and it is probably accurate to say that the most rapid progress is possible by a modification of environment accompanied by a decreasing, but not too rapidly decreasing, system of control. If the problem could be kept upon the plane of pure reason, it would still be a large problem, but it would be simplicity itself in comparison with the practical problem which confronts the world at the present time. Each one of the factors is itself the battlefield of warring interests. Governmental systems seem to have a life of their own, with all the determination of the living organism to maintain its existence. The decay of doctrinal religion has to a large extent deprived humanity of any clear objective, attainable or otherwise, and it would appear that indirect progress, or the solution of the problems of life from day to day in the light of experience, is for the moment the only solid ground upon which to build.

At first sight this situation seems to lend powerful support to a policy of what in fact promises to be a world dictatorship. To those who have no practical experience of large organisations, which is in essence the position of bankers, there is an attractive logic about a world planned and controlled like a machine. But, in fact, society does not work like a machine, but like a living organism. Any works manager will testify that the surest and shortest method of bringing about what is called labour trouble, is to endeavour to organise his factory as if the difference between the tools and the men in it were merely a difference of degree. At the beginning of the European War in 1914, collectivism, which is clearly allied to this idea of a machine-organised world, was almost as prevalent amongst the executive and administrative grades of industry as amongst the manual workers. Four years of organisation under war conditions, which brought into being collectivist mechanism to an extent otherwise impossible, disillusioned both the worker and the technician, not so much as to the soundness of the theory regarded as a means of attaining maximum production, as in regard to its extreme social unattractiveness.

Italy and Russia have, since the European War, had their own special forms of collectivist organisation, which it would be absurd to denounce as having failed from the purely materialistic point of view. It would be equally untrue to suggest that in either of them is there any approach to general satisfaction with the type of civilisation to which they tend, and still less ground for supposing that the extension of the policy for which they both appear to stand, in the direction of a world state organised on the philosophy of the subservience of the individual to the organisation, would be likely to meet with any more general approbation. Without going too deeply into this aspect of the problem, it seems safe to suggest that the supposition that individuals can be regarded as units in the census figures and catered for on this basis, is a fundamental mistake not merely in ethics but in works management.

Only a cursory acquaintance with history is requisite to appreciate the fact that the major conflict of human existence is concerned with what we are accustomed to call liberty. Physical existence upon this planet requires the provision either by the individual himself, or by organised society, of bed, board, and clothes, and the maintenance and continuation of existence is the strongest force in human politics. There has never been a period of history in which this individual determination to live and to insure the continuance of human life has not been conditioned, not so much by physical facts, as by human action itself. The cave-man probably found his chief difficulty less in the lack of game, or in his peculiar housing problem arising from a shortage of eligible caves, than in the fact that his neighbour, instead of exploring new territory and finding an additional cave, preferred to take measures to expel him from the sites already developed. Not, I think, so much because he liked fighting, as for lack of ability to conceive of the existence of enough caves. Fundamentally there is little difference discernible in the outlook of man upon the situation to-day.

The world is obsessed, or possessed, by a scarcity complex. While at the date of writing Great Britain is preparing for another war, she still has a million unemployed, farms going out of cultivation and agricultural products being destroyed because they cannot be sold, publicists still inform us on the one hand that the situation is due to over-production, and on the other hand that sacrifices must be made by everyone, that we must all work harder, consume less, and produce more. Yet no economic training is necessary to assess the meaning of the existing situation. On the one hand we have an enormous and increasing capacity to produce the goods and services which are the *primary* objective of civilisation and which probably form the material basis on which alone a cultural super-structure can be reared. On the other hand we have an immense population not only unable to obtain from the shops, which are so anxious to sell, those goods which they are unable to buy, but are, by the miscalled unemployment problem, prevented from producing still further goods. Ordinary common sense alone seems to be required to recognise that only one thing stands between this practically unlimited capacity to produce, and what is in fact a definitely limited capacity to consume, and that is the money system, the bottle-neck which separates production and consumption.

Now the evidence is clear enough that this bottle-neck actually operates in fact to an extent exceeding that in which any control of economic process has operated before. He would, I think, be a bold protagonist of the existing financial system who would contend that the results are meeting with general approbation. Just to the extent that the conditions in the world have improved in the past few years—and it must be admitted that this extent is quite limited—this improvement has been obtained by forcibly depriving those persons who, by adherence to the rules of the financial system, had acquired sufficient purchasing power to release them from the pressure of the control, for the partial benefit of those not so fortunate. In passing it may be noted how the power of taxation has grown into a form of oppression beside which the modest efforts of the robber barons of the Middle Ages must appear crude. While the system is based fundamentally upon a theory of rewards and punishments, modern financial methods, in conjunction with the taxation system, would appear to suggest that the acquisition of the reward is proper ground for the imposition of punishment in the form of taxation which will distribute the reward amongst those who have not worked for it. I have very little doubt that in this we are witnessing not merely the decay of the financial system, but of the whole theory of rewards and punishments as applied to economics.

However this may be, the perfecting of the financial system of control outlined in the previous chapter has been contemporaneous with a rising wave of discontent and disillusionment, and it is obvious enough that competent financial policy as operated by those in present control of the financial system aims not so much at removing this discontent, as at removing all mechanism by which it could be made effective. That is the objective of the disarmament propaganda in its various forms. So that we seem to be in possession of a certain amount of preliminary evidence which would weigh against this centralised control of finance. A further examination, I am afraid, only strengthens this view.

Mention has been made of the outstanding prosperity in a material sense which was experienced by the population of the United States during the period 1921-1929. No serious effort has been made to deny the fact that this period was terminated by the action of the Federal Reserve Banking System, partly by the raising of rates for call money to a fantastic figure, and partly by the calling in of loans irrespective of the interest rates offered. So far as any excuse is put forward for the action taken, it is that worse consequences than did in fact ensue would have been the result of further delay. Viewed in the light of subsequent effects it seems difficult to understand in what way this could have been true. Apart altogether from this, however, the course pursued strengthens the impression which is produced by an examination of the lesser financial crises which have been a feature of the twentieth century, that there is something in the banking system and its operation, which produces a constitutional inability to look at the industrial system as anything other than the basis of a financial system. To the banker, the satisfactory conditions of industry at any time are those which make the banking system work most smoothly. If it cannot be made to work smoothly, it must be made to work, even though in the process every other interest is sacrificed.

Only the exercise of a childlike faith, which

the present generation seems unlikely to supply, would secure agreement with the proposition that a system which has produced undesirable results in cumulative measure as its power increases, would produce better results if its power became absolute. While grave criticism of the personnel of the banking system and its prostitution to politics of a peculiarly vicious character is becoming daily more common and seems in many cases to be justified, it is evident that the world is becoming daily less willing to trust *any* personnel with a system at once so powerful, irresponsible, and convulsive in its operation.

While, as previously suggested, it is the reverse of true to accuse *financiers* of planning or desiring war, the financial *system*, of which they are the defenders, is, beyond question, the chief cause of international friction. Since, as we have seen, no nation can buy its own production, a struggle for markets in which to dispose of the surplus is inevitable. The translation of this commercial struggle into a military contest is merely a question of time and opportunity.

CHAPTER VIII

THE CAUSES OF WAR

PERHAPS the first necessity, if we wish to arrive at the truth of this matter, is to be clear on what we mean by "war". The technical definition of war is "any action taken to impose your will upon an enemy, or to prevent him from imposing his will upon you". It will be recognised at once that this definition of war makes the motive rather than the method the important matter to consider. More energy is devoted at the present time to the endeavour to modify the *methods* of war than to removing the *motive* for war. If we recognise this, we shall be in a better position to realise that we are never at peace —that only the form of war changes.

Military wars are waged by nations, a statement which is the basis for the somewhat naïve and, I think, certainly erroneous idea that you would abolish war if you abolished nations. This is much like saying that you would abolish rate-paying if you abolished Urban District Councils. You do not dispose of a problem by enlarging its boundaries, and, if I am not mistaken, the seeds of war are in every village.

We can get a glimpse of the main causes of war if we consider the problems of statesmen, who are expected to guide the destinies of nations. I suppose most statesmen at the present time would agree that their primary problem is to increase employment, and to induce trade prosperity for their own nationals, and there are few of them who would not add that the shortest way to achieve this would be to capture foreign markets. Once this, the common theory of international trade, is assumed, we have set our feet upon a road whose only end is war. The use of the word "capture" indicates the desire to take away from some other country, something with which it being unable, also, to be prosperous without general employment, does not desire to part. That is endeavouring to impose your will upon an adversary, and is economic war, and economic war has always resulted in military war, and probably always will.

The so-called psychological causes of war are the response of human nature to irritations which can be traced to this cause either directly or indirectly. To say that all men will fight if sufficiently irritated seems to me to be an argument against irritating them, rather than against human nature. It is not the irritation which causes the economic war, it is the economic war which causes the irritation. Military war is an intensification of economic war, and differs only in method and not in principle. The armaments industry, for instance, provides employment and high wages to at least the same extent that it provides profits to employers, and I cannot see any difference between the culpability of the employee and that of the employer. I have no interest, direct or indirect, in the armaments industry, but I am fairly familiar with Big Business, and I do not believe that the bribery and corruption, of which we have heard so much in connection with armaments, is any worse in that trade than in any other.

So long, then, as we are prepared to agree, firstly, that the removal of industrial unemployment is the primary object of statesmanship, and, secondly, that the capture of foreign markets is the shortest path to the attainment of this objective, we have the primary economic irritant to military war always with us, and, moreover, we have it in an accelerating rate of growth, because production is expanding through the use of power machinery, and undeveloped markets are contracting. Any village which has two grocery shops, each competing for an insufficient, and decreasing, amount of business, while continually enlarging its premises, is a working demonstration of the economic causes of war—is, in fact, itself at war by economic methods.

I do not believe that it is sensible to lecture the public of any or all of the nations on either the wickedness or the horrors of war, or to ask for goodwill to abolish military war or the trade in armaments, so long as it remains true that, if one of the village grocers captures the whole of the other grocer's business, the second grocer and his employees will suffer. Or if it remains true that if one nation captures the whole of another nation's trade the population of the second nation will be unemployed, and, being unemployed, they will suffer also. It is poverty and economic insecurity which submits human nature to the greatest strain, a statement which is easily provable by comparing suicide statistics with bankruptcy statistics and business depression. Suicides are less in number during wars, not because people like wars, but because there is more money about. Suicides are also less in number during trade booms for the same reason. To know, therefore, whether war is inevitable, we have to know whether, firstly, there is enough real wealth available to keep the whole population in comfort *without* the whole of the population being employed, and, secondly, if this is so, what it is that prevents this wealth from being distributed. In regard to the first question, I believe there can be no doubt as to the answer. We are all beginning to be familiar with the phrase "poverty amidst plenty", and it is generally admitted that the crisis of the past decade has been a crisis of glut and not a crisis of scarcity. Yet during that crisis, poverty has been widely extended, because *unemployment* has been widely extended. So that we have experimental evidence that full employment is not necessary to produce the wealth that we require—it is only necessary to the end that we may be able to distribute wages—quite a different matter. In regard to the second question, therefore, we know it is lack of money in the hands of individuals to enable them to buy the wealth which is available, and not the lack of available goods, which makes men poor. As our arrangements are at the present time, money is primarily distributed in respect of employment, which, as the glut has shown, is in many cases not necessary, or even desirable. So that it is not too much to say that the causes of war and the causes of poverty amidst plenty are the same, and they may be found in the monetary and wage system, and that broadly speaking the cure for poverty and the beginnings of the cure for war can be found in a simple rectification of the money

100

system.   This rectification must, I think, take the form of a National Dividend, either in a simple or more complex form, so that while there is *real wealth* to be distributed, nobody shall lack for want of *money* with which to buy.   It has already been shown that money is actually *made* by the banking system, and not by agriculture or industry.   The "Encyclopaedia Britannica" states the matter clearly in its article on banking in the words: "Banks lend money by *creating* the means of payment out of nothing."

It seems difficult to make it clear that the proposal for a National Dividend, which would enable the products of our industrial system to be bought by our own population, has nothing to do with Socialism, as that is commonly understood.   The main idea of Socialism appears to be the nationalisation of productive undertakings and their administration by Government departments.   Whatever merits such a proposal may have, or may not have, it does not touch the difficulty we have been considering.

The provision of a National Dividend is

101

merely to place in the hands of each one of the population, in the form of dividend-paying shares, a share of what is now known as the National Debt, without, however, confiscating that which is already in private hands, since the National Credit, is, in fact immensely greater than that portion of the National Debt which now provides incomes to individuals.

The practical effect of a National Dividend would be, firstly, to provide a secure source of income to individuals which, though it might be desirable to augment it by work, when obtainable, would, nevertheless, provide all the necessary purchasing power to maintain self-respect and health. By providing a steady demand upon our producing system, it would go a long way towards stabilising business conditions, and would assure producers of a constant home market for their goods. We already have the beginnings of such a system in our various pension schemes and unemployment insurance, but the defect for the moment of these is that they are put forward in conjunction with schemes of taxation which go a long way towards neutralising their beneficial effect. While this is inevitable under our present monetary system, it is far from being inevitable when the essentially public nature of the monetary system receives the recognition which is its due, but is not yet admitted by our bankers.

It may be asked, with reason, why the provision of a National Dividend, even if effective in removing the prime motive for aggressive war on the part of Great Britain, would so affect the motives of other nations as to prevent them from making war upon us. I think the answer to this is twofold. In the first place, I believe it to be, while the present financial system persists, merely sentimental to suppose that a weak nation, particularly if it be also a rich nation, is a factor making for peace. Quite the contrary. It is as sensible to say that a bank would never be robbed if it had paper walls. International bankers are, almost to a man, strong advocates of national disarmament, but their bank clerks, alone amongst civilian employees in this country, are armed with revolvers, and the

103

strength of bank premises compares with that of modern fortresses. Strength, unaccompanied by a motive for aggression, is a factor making for peace. A radical modification of the existing financial system will make it possible to build up a strong and united nation free from economic dissension, which would, by its strength, offer a powerful deterrent to aggressive war. And, secondly the spectacle of a contented and prosperous Britain, willing to trade but not forced by unemployment to *fight* for trade, would provide an irresistible object-lesson in genuine progress and would be imitated everywhere.

Why should these modifications not be made? For an answer to that question I must refer you to the Bank of England, which is all-powerful in these matters. Mr. Montagu Norman, the Governor of the Bank of England, which is a private company, described the relations of the Bank of England and the Treasury as those of Tweedledum and Tweedledee.

It is not suggested that bankers have a wish to precipitate war. Far from it. Bankers dislike war only less than they dislike any change in a financial system with which, almost alone amongst other sections of the community, they appear to be completely satisfied.

CHAPTER IX

DIVIDENDS FOR ALL

WHILE the financial control of industry when inaugurated seems definitely undesirable, certain reservations will at once occur to the student. Industry has run riot over the countryside. A population which has been educated in the fixed idea that the chief, if not the only, objective of life is well named "business", whose politicians and preachers exhort their audiences to fresh efforts for the capture of markets and the provision of still more business, cannot be blamed if, as opportunity occurs, it still further sacrifices the amenities of the countryside to the building of more blast-furnaces and chemical works. Since the control of credit is the most perfect mechanism for the control of industrial activity, its use in the hands of a representative organisation would appear to be the best possible way of reducing the

THE MONOPOLY OF CREDIT

chaos which exists, to something like order.

The banking organisation at present existing, even if we are prepared to concede to it an altruism not particularly noticeable, is by its expressed philosophy seriously handicapped in dealing with this situation. This philosophy exalts industrial work to an end in itself, and deplores, as one of the major evils of the time, the leisure which it labels "the unemployment problem." While it possesses the power to inaugurate and modernise the plant of industry, and in the process to locate it geographically in accordance with the best interests of the community, the carrying out of such a policy must of necessity be entrusted to technically capable individuals. Unfortunately for the banking system, these individuals cannot be restrained from making each successive plan more efficient than the last, with the result that a given output requires less and less labour, and the unemployment problem, as labelled, is thereby increasingly complicated. Only by a frenzied acceleration of capital sabotage, which is now being openly advocated in many quarters, can the population (which would, so far as the physical aspect of the situation is concerned, be free to enjoy the product of the plants already existing) be kept at work on the production of capital goods.

It would appear, therefore, that even this desirable aspect of financial control is rendered ineffective under its present operation. Before an intelligent system of regional planning can be inaugurated with any hope of success, some agreement is necessary as to whether unemployment, in its alternative description of leisure, is a misfortune or whether it is a release. If it is a release, then obviously it must not be accompanied by economic, or rather financial, penalisation. If it is a misfortune, then clearly every effort should be directed to restraining the abilities of those engineers and organisers who are prepared to make not two, but two hundred blades of grass grow where one grew before.

An appreciation of this position is perhaps the shortest way to arrive at a conception of the modifications which are required. If we assume that the constant efforts to reduce the amount of labour per unit of production are justified, and we recognise the unquestionable fact that the genuine consumptive capacity of the individual is limited, we must recognise that the world, whether consciously or not, is working towards the Leisure State. The production system under this conception would be required to produce those goods and services which the consumer desires of it with a minimum and probably decreasing amount of human labour. Production, and still more the activities which are commonly referred to as "business," would of necessity cease to be the major interest of life and would, as has happened to so many biological activities, be relegated to a position of minor importance, to be replaced, no doubt, by some form of activity of which we are not yet fully cognisant.

In a physical sense then we should be living in a world in which economic processes were carried out by two agencies, one, as heretofore, the agency of individual effort and from an economic point of view of decreasing importance, and the other, as the result of the plant, organisation, and knowledge which are the cumulative result of the effort not only of the present generation, but of the pioneers and inventors of the past. This second agency can, of course, be collectively described as real (as distinct from financial) capital. Now it is quite easy to make out a perfectly simple ethical justification for the proposition that the share of the product due to the individual under such a state of affairs would be (1) a small and decreasing share due to his individual efforts, and (2) a large and increasing amount due to his rights as a shareholder or an inheritor, or if it may be preferred, a tenant for life of the communal capital. But in fact such an argument is far less satisfactory than the equally valid argument that the communal capital is useless to exactly the extent that any proportion of the public is prevented from drawing upon it, which is, of course, the general explanation of the vast amount of idle real wealth at the present day.

Up to this point the facts must be clear enough to anyone who is content to consider the matter dispassionately. Proceeding from this stage, and remembering that a satisfactory financial system is simply a reflection in figures of a state of affairs alleged to exist in fact, or is, in other words, simply an accounting system, it is not difficult to understand that wages and salaries in relation to dividends ought to become increasingly unimportant. Production is far more dependent upon real capital than it is upon labour, although without labour there is no production. More and more the position of labour, using, of course, this word in its widest possible sense, tends to become the catalyst in an operation impossible without its presence, but carried on with a decreasing direct contribution from labour itself.

Let us at this point for the sake of clarity identify the community with the nation and in doing so be careful not to confuse administration with ownership. It ought not to be difficult to see that a situation which may truly be described as revolutionary is disclosed. In place of the relation of the individual to the nation being that of a taxpayer it is easily seen to be that of a shareholder. Instead of paying for the doubtful privilege of being entitled to a particular brand of passport, its possession entitles him to draw a dividend, certain, and probably increasing, from the past and present efforts of the community of which he is a member. The National Debt, which he did not create, becomes a national credit which is a reflection of the national capital which he did create. His budget is not required to balance because his wealth is always increasing. He does not require to fight for foreign markets, since obtaining foreign markets merely means a longer working day. Having more leisure he is less likely to suffer from either individual or national nerve-strain, and having more time to meet his neighbours can reasonably be expected to understand them more fully. Not being dependent upon a wage or salary for subsistence, he is under no necessity to suppress his individuality, with the result that his capacities are likely to take new forms of which we have so far little conception.

CHAPTER X

CONCLUSION

SINCE at the time at which these lines are written the world is universally, if not uniformly, involved in a major crisis, it is perhaps useful to consider not alone what ought to be done (since it is hoped that at any rate in outline the nature of the disease will have become evident from the preceding pages, while the principles of the remedy may be gathered from the appendices and from previous works), but what in fact can be done.

Perhaps the first point on which to be clear is that this immense, nay, almost omnipotent, power which is wielded by the financial organisation, and which therefore must in the nature of things be responsible for the situation in the world to-day, has not until recently been recognised in its true nature. In fact, every artifice, either of the press or of politics, has been used to identify the conduct of nations

115

with their titular governments, while at the same time vilifying them for the progressively disastrous results.

It is, in my opinion, not too much to say that these governments are now superseded by financial institutions, and that these financial institutions, so far as can be humanly judged, are in an impregnable position.

Now if we have an undertaking of which the directorate cannot be removed, however at variance with the desires of the proprietors may be its conduct, we can see that the outcome must be one of two things. Either the directors will, by superior adjustments of policy, produce such results as will in time remove cause for complaint, or alternatively, their policy being bad, the undertaking will go to shipwreck. In these circumstances there is probably only one useful course of action, and that is, so far as possible, to make it clear to everyone concerned that in existing circumstances the directors cannot be removed, and that they alone are responsible for the outcome of their policy.

That, I think is the course which at the

present time should be consistently pursued. It seems difficult to doubt that the efforts of those in control of financial policy are primarily, if not entirely, concerned with making the world safe for bankers, rather than making the world safe. By one of those curious ironies which seem to be present in great crises, it happens, as one might say, by a side-wind, that the world cannot be made safe without removing the banker, painlessly or otherwise, from the commanding position which he now occupies. The alternative is in fact clear, and nothing effective can be done to protect civilisation from its major risks which is not an attack upon the power of finance. It would seem, therefore, that the fixation of responsibility largely by means of an explanation of financial processes, and of the probable results of financial policy, is the first effective step which can be taken, not only to prepare for the still further chaos which seems likely to ensue, but to strengthen the hands of those agencies which may be effective in the restoration of popular control.

But this fixation of responsibility can in no

117

sense be considered complete if it remains at this point. There probably never was within historic times so important a period in the world's history as that through which we are passing at the present time. If we are to emerge from this period into the millenium which is easily possible, although by no means certain, the reorganisation necessary must be based on a philosophy which, whatever other elements it may contain, will certainly not enthrone the productive and industrial systems in the preponderatingly important position which they have occupied for the past hundred years. A perusal of contemporary journalism, nay, an examination of the formal constitutions of such States as those of Italy and the Soviet Republics of Russia, would lead one to suppose that the sole object of man's existence is material production. The matter has been well put in the doggerel, "We go to work to earn the cash to buy the food to get the strength to go to work to earn the cash . . ."; and so *ad infinitum*. For this reason it is necessary to examine any proposal for the rectification of the existing situation with at least as much care as the policy now operative.

Another aspect of this same mentality is exemplified by the arrogation to themselves, by labour movements in particular, of the freehold rights of all civic virtue. There is probably no subject in which there is more muddled thinking than in respect to the right of the unfortunate in this world on the one hand to compassion, and on the other hand to consultation. There cannot be too much concern for the unfortunate condition of large numbers of human beings in contemporary society, but to suppose that this position gives them a special claim to exercise a voice in the direction of affairs is to put a premium on inexperience irrespective of whether the conditions which have brought about that inexperience are personal or otherwise. The modern State is a completely immoral organisation. Its taxation differs in no fundamental quality from that levied by a highwayman of the Middle Ages, and the fact that a small proportion of the taxes which are exacted is used for the alleviation of the more pressing

119

necessities of the poor, bears much the same relation to the question as the liberality, to his followers, of a mountain bandit. Political democracy *without* economic democracy is dynamite. The need is to abolish poverty, not to represent it.

It seems indisputable that no modern economic system can be based on any theory of rewards and punishments. Either the economic system will provide, as it undoubtedly can, an ample living for everyone, in which case arbitrary restriction, even if practicable, would appear to be quite senseless, or, on the other hand, some method at present quite unknown must be developed for dealing with a situation in which there is, for instance, one post in the economic system to be filled, and ten equally satisfactory applicants for it. Failure to deal with this latter situation makes a complete reconstruction of human nature indispensable, and the reconstruction of human nature within a reasonable period does not appear to be a hopeful undertaking.

If civilisation is not to disappear altogether, there will within a comparatively short period of time arise a situation in which bankers as at present understood will be replaced. It seems important to recognise that when this situation does arise it will be just as easy to inaugurate a financial system which will meet all the necessities of a modern civilisation, as to introduce piecemeal reforms. Here again there is much evidence of inability to think clearly on the matter. Numbers of well-disposed people recognise the implacable hostility with which effective proposals are met, and are tempted to say in effect "we cannot do the right thing, let us at any rate do something". Although it seems difficult to obtain general understanding of it, fundamentally a financial system is a matter of pure arithmetic, and the results which will be obtained depend entirely upon the arithmetical factors which are employed and only to a very temporary extent on the particular brand of black magic which is superimposed. Whatever may be the case in other matters, compromise in arithmetic seems singularly out of place, and it is much better that the present defective system should be allowed to discredit its upholders, and so render genuine reconstruction possible, than that an alternative, of which the effects are not sufficiently beneficial as to place it at once in an impregnable position, should be substituted for it.

COMMITTEE ON FINANCE AND INDUSTRY

Chairman : LORD MACMILLAN
Statement of Evidence submitted before the Committee, May 1st, 1930

By C. H. DOUGLAS

SUMMARY OF EVIDENCE TO BE OFFERED

(1) That the primary cause of the industrial depression and consequent unrest is financial. It is due to lack of power to buy, not due to lack of either power or will to produce. That is to say, it is not in the main administrative, nor due to the technical relationship between employers and employed, but is due to money relationships which are governed primarily by the financial system, and, secondarily, by financial policy. Such "remedies" as "rationalisation" or "nationalisation" do not touch the fundamental problem.

123

(2) That while the policy pursued in regard to credit issue probably controls the general rate of production, and may be the main cause of the differential rate of economic prosperity as between one nation and another, the fundamental defect of the financial system, as operated, is mathematical, not political. The existing financial system is not a correct reflection of economic fact, as it should be, and is both misleading and restrictive.

(3) Any effective remedy must traverse the claim of the banking system to the ownership of the financial credit extended to industry, a claim which is implied by the fact that at present money, constituting in the main new purchasing power, is loaned to a bank's customers, not given.

SECTION I

It may be helpful to define the phrases used in the preceding proposition.

(1) *Industrial Depression.*—Industrial depression may be characterised as a lack of sufficient orders to keep both plant and

personnel employed, together with an accompanying lowering of the price level in relation to the cost of production, so that both the manufacturer fails to make a profit and the volume of wages of the wage-earning class tends to fall. The phenomena are cumulative and have no relation either to productive capacity or psychological demand. The material by-products are bankruptcies, the breaking-up of plant, and the psychological by-products are industrial and political unrest and the destruction of social morale.

(2) *Power to Buy.*—Power to buy consists in the ability to offer what the seller requires in exchange for his goods, i.e. money.

(3) *Finance.*—Finance in its relation to industry may be defined as the provision of the monetary inducement to deliver goods and services. It is obviously the same thing as power to buy. It is proposed to prove that with negligible exceptions, power to buy originates and is vested in the banking system.

(4) *Financial System.*—This may be considered as having three parts, the credit issue system, the price system, and the taxation system.

125

(*a*) The credit issue system may be considered as predominantly made up of two principal factors, bank loans and the discounting of bills. Since the result of both of these is to swell both the assets and the liabilities of a bank's accounts, they may for the purpose of this investigation be treated as similar.

(*b*) The price system is founded in the main on two propositions. Firstly, that all costs of production must go into prices. Cost, therefore, forms the lower limit of prices. Secondly, that the price of an article is what it will fetch, that is to say, the major limit of prices is governed by the ability and willingness of the purchaser to buy. It should be noted that while there is no major limit to prices, business cannot under existing conditions be carried on with prices below cost. Any attempt to do this consists, in essence, in the provision of a credit subsidy by the seller in aid of a reduction of prices below cost.

(*c*) The taxation system is preferably considered in conjunction with the alternate method of providing money for public expenditure, which is by means of loans. The inducement to subscribe to a loan consists in the interest paid on it, and in the varying terms of redemption. Taxation may properly be considered as being a forced non-repayable, recurring "loan", a portion of the proceeds of which are used to pay the inducement offered to a voluntary loan. It is of importance to note that while the physical effects of spending money raised by taxation are exactly similar to those of spending money raised by a loan, in the latter case a financial asset is created, whereas in case of taxation no financial asset is created. One result of this is that, for instance, in Great Britain there is nothing corresponding to a capital account, its place being taken by the National Debt.

(5) *Financial Policy.*—Financial Policy may be defined as an endeavour to vary within the limits of the preceding definitions, both the volume of credit issue, and as a result of the second canon of the price system, the level of prices. It should be noted that while prices may be driven down by financial policy to the cost of production, financial policy does not *directly* affect the *cost* of production other

127

than by producing conditions which may induce workmen to accept lower wages, and by the imposition of taxes which go into costs. The result, however, of financial policy directed to lowering *prices* within the existing financial system is to discourage production, and by causing a relative rise in overhead charges and a smaller volume of production may actually result in raising the minimum price level.

Argument. Section I

(1) I. In order to distinguish the artificial condition known as "industrial depression" from the underlying physical facts, it is perhaps desirable to survey the physical position of industry. It will be admitted that the ostensible objective of industry is the production for use of goods and services to an extent rendered possible by the progress of the industrial arts. The physical factors in the attainment of this objective consist of what are commonly called raw materials, which may be reasonably defined as materials in the state in which they are found in nature, the application to these raw materials of a

128

process involving, in the broad sense, tools, and thirdly, the expenditure of energy. The distinguishing characteristic of the nineteenth and twentieth centuries is the rapid advance of process together with the rendering available of large amounts of energy, which may be considered as derived from the sun, through the various agencies of coal, oil, steam, etc. It appears to be reasonably true to say, that for a given process the rate of production is proportionate to the rate of use of energy, and to a large extent it is immaterial whether this energy is muscular or is applied by machines. The physical effect of these factors has therefore been to increase the rate of production of a given article per human unit of labour. For instance, the rate of production of pig-iron is three times as great per man employed as it was in 1914. A workman using automatic machines can make 4,000 glass bottles as quickly as he could have made 100 by hand twenty-five years ago. In 1919 the index of factory output (based upon 1914 as 100) was 147, and the index of factory employment was 129. By 1927 output had risen to 170, but employment had sunk to 115. In 1928 American farmers were using 45,000 harvesting and threshing machines, and with them had displaced 130,000 farm hands. In automobiles, output per man has increased to 310 per cent, an increase of 210 per cent.

(2) I. It will probably be admitted that the power and will to produce are sufficiently demonstrated in the foregoing considerations. It would not be seriously contested that the psychological will to buy does not exist, and it seems beyond dispute, therefore, ·that the reason that buying up to the power of the ability of the industrial system to produce does not take place is because there is a lack of money required to pay the prices demanded. In a subsequent section it is proposed to prove that under the existing financial system the general public can at no time acquire by purchase the whole of production, but while this is so, and the *proportion of a given volume* of production which the public *can* buy is probably fixed by the system, *the total volume of production* is almost certainly governed by financial policy.

(3) I. In order to fix responsibility for this policy it is, perhaps, only necessary to quote a recent speech by Mr. Montagu Norman, Governor of the Bank of England, as reported in *The Times* of March 21st, 1930. A previous speaker, Mr. Hargraves, had said, "They held the hegemony, so far as this country was concerned, in finance, and he thought he might say, considering the way in which they were regarded in foreign countries, that they also held the hegemony of the world." Mr. Montagu Norman commented, "He was glad to note what Mr. Hargraves said about the hegemony in one place and another. He believed it was largely true, so far as overseas were concerned, and if it was true, it was largely the result of work which the Bank had devoted, first of all, to the stabilisation of Europe, and, secondly, to the relationships between the central banks, which were originally advocated at Genoa." In this connection it is of practical importance, as bearing on the difficulties of obtaining an alteration in the financial system itself, to note that the spokesmen of orthodox finance seem to assume the

position of arbiters and protagonists of morals, both individual and international.

(4) I. Some indication of the practical effect of the admitted hegemony of Finance and its interpretation of its functions may be gained by a consideration of the results of some of its activities in the post-War period, and may be helpful.

Prior to its subjugation by the Financial Committee of the League of Nations, the following descriptions of affairs in Austria, taken from Colonel Repington's "After the War", is fairly typical.

"I am much impressed by studying the Austrian papers. They seem detached and indifferent about foreign affairs, but are full of accounts of all sorts of new or extended industries springing up, and I counted twenty-three pages of commercial advertisements in Sunday's *Neue Freie Presse*. I read or hear of every kind of old industry being extended, and of some new ones opened. New machinery is being employed, and on the farms prize stock are being bought and farm buildings improved by the rich peasants

132

who throve on the war. From Upper and Lower Austria, Styria, and the Tyrol it is all the same story of new developments, and what is really going on is an endeavour to make the new Austria less dependent on her neighbours, and less forced to buy abroad in markets made fearfully dear by the exchange. I find that two-thirds of the Austrian deficit is due to food subsidies, chiefly bread. A loaf of 1,260 grammes is now sold for nine kronen, but costs sixty kronen to the State. Even a Rothschild is paid, therefore, fifty-one kronen by the State for every loaf he eats."

Subsequent to the financial " stabilisation " of Austria, the correspondent of the *Observer*, writing on February 15th, 1925, states: " It is regrettable that the new wave of depression should have swept Vienna, to such an extent as to cause 149 cases of suicide during the past month."

The *New Republic* of New York, in its issue of December 3rd, 1924, states: "The League of Nations at its last meeting imposed severe restrictions (financial) on the Austrian Government. These circumstances have made living conditions worse than at any time since the collapse after the Armistice."

(5) I. On the other hand, in France, which was physically the severest sufferer by the War, there is no unemployment, and there has been no serious attempt at deflation. If we are to judge by such books as Monsieur Chastenet's "The Bankers' Republic", French finance is free from undue purism and from any assumption of moral leadership. In spite of this, however, the industrial situation is admittedly better in France than it is in this country, and what is perhaps equally important, the plant of France has been modernised to a much greater extent than has been possible in England in these times of stringency.

(6) I. The Curves attached to this section, indicate the business and psychological effect in Great Britain of the policy which has been pursued. During the period covered by the curve, in which the bankruptcies have risen from about 900 per annum to nearly 7,000[1] per annum, and the suicides have increased over the whole of the kingdom by 67 per cent

[1] This figure *includes* Scotland.

134

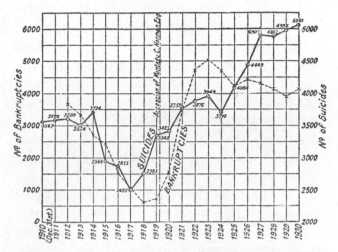

This graph is for England and Wales only, Scotland is omitted. Montagu Collett Norman, Esq., Governor, Bank of England, 1920. (Messrs. Brown, Shipley Co., U.S.A.)

The curves demonstrate in a remarkable manner the predominant effect of financial anxiety in contributing to despair and suicide. The deflationary policy of the Bank of England inaugurated in April, 1920 was immediately reflected in a rise during that year of bankruptcies from just over 700 to just over 1,500. During the ten years in which this policy has been in operation bankruptcies per annum have increased by 600 per cent and suicides by nearly 100 per cent.

per annum, and in Scotland by 100 per cent, every large bank in Great Britain has maintained, or increased its dividend, has enormously expanded its premises, and placed large sums to its visible reserve, and created still larger invisible reserves, and this in spite of the enormous losses alleged to have been made in respect of loans to industry.

During the same period of time the greater proportion of the larger industrial undertakings have passed from the possession of those who originally initiated and financed them into the control of banks and finance houses.

It would appear a somewhat remarkable comment on this situation that the spokesmen of the Bank of England, so far from expressing any regret, appear to regard the results obtained as being a proper subject for self-congratulation.

In considering the policy pursued by this Institution and its obvious subservience to the Federal Reserve Board of the U.S.A., it is difficult to avoid the conclusion that it has come under the control of influences definitely hostile to the continued influence of Great Britain and (possibly under cover of paranoiac schemes for world reorganisation on a financial basis) has been a chief agent in the industrial

136

demoralisation and social disillusionment which are now general.

Section II
Argument. Section II

(1) II. In Section I it has been suggested that a state of industrial depression which may be considered to be synonymous with a condition of slackened production, arises primarily from financial and not from physical or psychological causes, and specifically from lack of effective demand, that is to say, from the difficulty of obtaining orders backed by the power to pay in money. If this be admitted, it is incontestable that any measures which increase the amount of money available to back orders will increase the rate of production, and conversely, any measures which decrease the amount of money available to back orders will decrease production. It is perhaps unnecessary before this Committee to go over the ground which has been so ably covered by one of its members, the Right Honourable R. McKenna, to the effect that the main cause of

137

the increase or decrease in the amount of money available at any time may be found in banking policy, and notably in central banking policy. Mr. McKenna's argument may be epitomised in the statement that "every bank loan creates a deposit and the repayment of every bank loan destroys a deposit." Since, rather surprisingly, there are certain orthodox economists who are not prepared to admit this statement, I attach a simple mathematical proof which would appear to put the matter outside the range of discussion.

Let Deposits $= D$
Let Loans $= L$
Let Cash in Hand $= C$
Let Capital $= K$

Then :

Assets $= L + C$
Liabilities $= D + K$

So that:

$$L + C = D + K$$

Differentiating with respect to time we have:

$$\frac{dL}{dt} + \frac{dC}{dt} = \frac{dD}{dt}, \text{ K being fixed } \frac{dK}{dt} = 0$$

Assuming cash to be kept fixed $\dfrac{dC}{dt} = 0$

Therefore $\dfrac{dL}{dt} = \dfrac{dD}{dt}.$

(2) II. It would, perhaps, be misleading to describe this ingenious process as wholesale counterfeiting, as since the Bank Act of 1928 the State has resigned its sovereign rights over Finance in favour of the international private organisation known as the Bank of England.

(3) II. Since 1920 the policy pursued in Great Britain under the leadership of the Bank of England has been continuously restrictive, that is to say, directed to the reduction of the amount of money available to back orders. This policy has been termed "deflationary," but it is open to considerable doubt whether the term is justified. It is applicable, correctly, to a situation in which prices and money are decreased in such a manner that the purchasing power of the unit of money rises in the same proportion that its total quantity is decreased. This

condition has not been fulfilled, as the amount of money in the hands of the public has been decreased by taxation and by other methods at considerably greater rate than prices have fallen. While the upper limit of prices follows approximately the quantity theory of money, the lower limit is governed by cost of production. The outcome of this set of circumstances has been to restrict production, to force down the price of real property, and to enrich the moneylenders and insurance companies at the expense of the individual and the producer.

(4) II. To indicate the divergence between the policy which has been pursued in this country and, for instance, the United States since 1920, it is perhaps sufficient to note that the increase in the total deposits of the London Clearing Banks for the six years ending October, 1928, was only £16,000,000, to a total of £1,790,000,000. In contrast with this, the increase in the deposits of the Member Banks of the Federal Reserve system, over the same period of time, was £1,873,000,000, or £83,000,000 more of an *increase* than the *total deposits* in the British banks. It is not nec-

essary, I think, to seek further for the cause of the disparity in material and industrial prosperity between this country and the United States in the post-war period.

(5) II. It is not suggested, however, that the difficulties inherent in the existing financial system have been solved to any considerable extent in the United States, but it seems incontestable that physical assets (which must form the basis of material prosperity under any financial system) have been increased in the United States, and their production retarded in Great Britain simultaneously, with a corresponding effect on the morale, of the people concerned. The possibility of manipulating the economic prosperity as between one country and another through an international financial organisation, such as is growing up independent of effective national control, and having ends to serve which are not those of the populations affected, is perhaps one of the most serious aspects of the annexation of financial credit. It is at one and the same time rendered possible and condemned to catastrophe by the circumstance

that it operates to produce a permanent and increasing disparity between the minimum collective price of products of the industrial system within a given credit area, and the collective, effective demand available for the goods so produced.

(6) II. The causes of this disparity are complex, but the two more important are (*a*) the "double circuit" of money in industry (*b*) the reinvestment of savings.

(*a*) The double circuit difficulty has been stated by me in the form of a proposition, which has been popularly known as the *A* plus *B* theorem. A factory or other productive organisation has, besides its economic function as a producer of goods, a financial aspect—it may be regarded on the one hand as a device for the distribution of purchasing power to individuals, through the media of wages, salaries, and dividends; and on the other hand as a manufactory of prices—financial values. From this standpoint its payments may be divided into two groups.

Group A.—All payments made to individuals (wages, salaries, and dividends).

Group B.—All payments made to other organisations (raw materials, bank charges, and other external costs.)

Now the rate of flow of purchasing power to individuals is represented by *A*, but since all payments go into prices, the rate of flow of prices cannot be less than *A* plus *B*. Since *A* will not purchase *A* plus *B*, a proportion of the product at least equivalent to *B* must be distributed by a form of purchasing power which is not comprised in the description grouped under *A*.

The above proposition is perhaps most simply grasped by recognising that the *B* payments may be considered in the light of the repayment of a bank loan by all the concerns to whom they are made, with the result involved in the relationship previously discussed between bank deposits and bank loans. When real capital (i.e. tools, etc.) is financed from savings, that condition is complicated by (*b*).

(*b*) The persistence of the idea that monetary saving has a physical counterpart in physical accumulation will no doubt exercise the attention of historians of the present period. Since money is normally distributable only through the agency of wages, salaries, and dividends, it being assumed that the interest on Government loans is provided by taxation, the whole of these wages, salaries, and dividends must have appeared in the cost, and consequently in the price of articles produced. It does not appear to need any elaborate demonstration to see that any saving of these wages, salaries, and dividends means that a proportion of the goods in the prices of which they appear as costs, must remain unsold within the credit area in which they are produced and are therefore, in the economic sense wasted. The investment of the funds so saved means the reappearance of the same sum of money in a fresh set of prices, so that on each occasion that a given sum of money is reinvested, a fresh set of price values is created without the creation of fresh purchasing power.

It will be evident that the processes just indicated are at the core of the problem under consideration and that a more exhaustive examination of them than is desirable in this survey, is imperative. The present intention is merely to emphasise their existence and importance.

Section III

(1) III. From Section II it would appear indisputable that all but an insignificant amount of effective demand is dependent for its financial component on bank loans in various forms. It will be hardly necessary to remark that the only value of these bank credits is contingent on the willingness of the industrial community to produce and supply goods and services in exchange for them. While it is conceivable that an industrial system might operate without money, it is inconceivable that a money system could operate without an industrial system.

(2) III. Financial credit, therefore, may be considered as a reflection of real credit, which is a measure of the capacity to produce and deliver goods and services, as, when, and where required. Since this conception of real credit implies an organised, orderly, and stable community, whose objective in production is

145

consumption, it seems difficult to object to the statement that the real basis of credit is the producing and consuming capacity of the community, and still more difficult to justify a condition of affairs in which this credit is loaned to it as an act of grace, although a charge for its mobilisation can easily be admitted. It is practically, however, more important to realise that a financial system which separates the ownership of credit from the community is self-destructive, since only the community has the requisite consuming power to maintain production at its maximum.

(3) III. In order to realise this, it is only necessary to bear in mind that money and credit are interchangeable, and that the definition of money is "any medium which no matter of what it is made, or why people want it, no one will refuse in exchange for his goods" (Professor Walker). Since the creation of financial credit is a costless proceeding in itself, the mechanical portion of the process merely consisting of writing figures in a book, and since financial credit arises out of this book-keeping technique, and is by definition

146

practically the only effective demand for goods and services, it is plain that the whole of the goods and services produced by the community are the potential property of the financial system as at present operated. The financial system as such, however, is incapable of of absorbing any considerable proportion of the possible production of the community, although it must be admitted that the proportion of branch banks to new houses in the past ten years shows a painstaking effort in this dircction. It is not therefore necessary to labour the fact that the identification of the credit now claimed by the banking system, with the general community, is an essential to the equation of effective demand with productive capacity.

(4) III. In the future attempts which will be made to give effect to such propositions as the foregoing, it will be necessary carefully to distinguish between the private administration of credit as a public property and what is commonly called "public administration," it being quite probable that the former is in every way preferable as a means of administration.

147

It may, perhaps, be permissible to quote from a book which has aroused considerable attention on the Continent, by the late Doctor Steiner, in this connection:

"Modern socialism is absolutely justified in demanding that the present-day methods under which production is carried on for individual profit, should be replaced by others, under which production is carried on for the sake of the common consumption. But it is just the person who most thoroughly recognises the justice of this demand who will find himself unable to concur in the conclusion which modern socialism deduces: That, therefore, the means of production must be transferred from private to communal ownership. Rather he will be forced to a conclusion that is quite different, namely: That whatever is privately produced by means of individual energies and talents must find its way to the community through the right channels."

(5) III. Since it is quite probable that the

time has not arrived at which it is practicable to obtain recognition of the contention advanced in this section, it would, no doubt, be premature to put forward any constructive proposals which involve its acceptance.

It is impossible that individual business will, after the experience of the post-war period, be content to work with bank loans which are liable to call at the most inconvenient moment, and there is evidence of an increasing disinclination to take all the risk and responsibility in collaboration with institutions possessing neither technical knowledge nor common interest with the individual enterprise. No doubt an appreciation of this situation has a good deal to do with the intensive propaganda for "rationalisation," jointly with a genuine inability to apprehend the fact that the "efficiency" of very large undertakings is a paper efficiency based on access to credit, bulk buying, and price making, and in many cases has no physical basis, the genuine efficiency of the smaller undertaking being frequently higher.

ADDENDA

The general principles required of any financial system sufficiently flexible to meet the conditions which now exist and to continue to reflect the economic facts as these facts change under the influence of improved process and the increased use of power, are simple and may be summarised as follows:

(*a*) That the cash credits of the population of any country shall at any moment be collectively equal to the collective cash prices for consumable goods for sale in that country (irrespective of the cost prices of such goods), and such cash credits shall be cancelled or depreciated only on the purchase or depreciation of goods for consumption.

(*b*) That the credits required to finance production shall be supplied not from savings, but be new credits relating to new production, and shall be recalled only in ratio of general depreciation to general appreciation.

(*c*) That the distribution of cash credits to individuals shall be progressively less dependent upon employment. That is to say, that the dividend shall progressively displace the wage and salary, as productive capacity increases per man-hour.

It seems quite possible that the form of organisation which would easily adapt itself to the embodiment of the foregoing principles would be that of a limited company. "Great Britain Limited" as a beginning for the "British Empire Limited" might form an organisation in which natural-born British subjects would be bond-holders. An elaboration of this conception would enable a transition to be made without shock and without any alteration in the existing administration of industry.

151

WORLD ENGINEERING CONGRESS TOKYO, 1929

THE APPLICATION OF ENGINEERING METHODS TO FINANCE

(Paper No. 685)

By C. H. Douglas, M.I.Mech.E.

In defining the profession of engineering as the application of the forces of nature to the uses of man, the Institution of Civil Engineers no doubt had in mind those forces which at the present time we are accustomed to call physical forces. There is no reason to limit the definition of such forces, and it is becoming increasingly recognised that the province of the engineer, and in particular the scope of the engineering method, can with advantage be extended to cover forces of a more metaphysical and psychological character.

153

Assuming that there is reason to bring the financial system under review, on the ground that it is not operating satisfactorily, and that, being in essence a combination of an enlarged Works Order and Distribution System combined with a metaphysical scheme for the mobilisation of human activities, it is at any rate interesting to consider the matter from an engineering point of view, and stripped of the emotional irrelevances with which it is frequently clothed.

In attacking an engineering problem the first point we settle, with as much exactness as possible, is our objective. No engineer observer of the discussions which take place in political and lay circles on the industrial problems of the present day can fail to be struck with the fact that the problem itself is rarely stated with any clearness. For instance, the paramount difficulty of the industrial system is commonly expressed as that of unemployment. Therefore the suggestion involved is that the industrial system exists to provide employment, and fails. Those who are engaged in the actual conduct of industry,

154

however, are specifically concerned to obtain a given output with a minimum of employment, and in fact, a decreasing amount of employment. Consequently, those who are talking about industry and those who are conducting industry have in their minds objectives which are diametrically opposed and incompatible. On the other hand, the great majority of those engaged in industry, anyhow, in its lower ranks, would claim that what they want from the industrial system is goods. Finally those whose interest in industry is purely financial, require from industry, simply, money.

We have, therefore, to recognise that there are at least three separate and distinct objectives alleged in the industrial system—

(1) Employment (2) Goods and services (3) Money.

(1) *Employment as the Objective of the Industrial System.*—For a given programme of production and a given standard of development of the industrial arts, output is proportionate to the energy employed in industry. Broadly speaking, the source of this energy is

155

immaterial. So much solar or mechanical energy, so much less human energy. If employment is accepted as the objective of the industrial system, therefore, and output to be a dependent variable of this objective, (a) either process and mechanical energy employed must be kept rigidly constant, or (b) output must be completely unfettered by any difficulties of sale.

(2) *Goods and Services as the Objective of the Industrial System.*—There are here two possible cases: (a) A fixed programme of production with unlimited improvement of process and employment of mechanical energy, resulting in a rapidly and constantly decreasing amount of employment in man-hours. (b) An advancing programme of production with unlimited improvement of process and employment of mechanical energy, resulting eventually in a saturated psychological demand, and automatically becoming similar to (a).

(3) *Money as the Objective of the Industrial System.*—It is perhaps only necessary to state this in brief form. Money is not made by

156

making or selling goods; it is made: (1) By digging gold, silver, and copper out of the earth and minting them. This represents perhaps 0.3 of 1 per cent of money in circulation. (2) By the printing of paper money, representing, perhaps, 10 per cent of the money in circulation. (3) The creation of credits by banks, representing, perhaps, 90 per cent of the money in circulation. With the exception of the labour employed in mining and working the metals in the first insignificant division, and the labour employed in the elaborate organisation of the banking system, the creation of money has nothing to do with the industrial system, although it represents an effective demand upon the whole product of the industrial system. The making of money as an objective of the industrial system, therefore, bears a close resemblance to Charles Lamb's method of obtaining roast pork by burning down the piggery.

Since money is not made by the industrial system, it is important to understand whence it originates and whither it eventually returns.

The matter has been epitomised in a short sentence by Mr. McKenna, Chairman of the Midland Bank: "Every loan creates a deposit, and the repayment of every loan destroys a deposit." The following explanation may make this clear to those who are not familiar with the technique, and who imagine that the money which banks loan to their customers is limited by the amount they receive from other customers. Imagine a new bank to be started —its so-called capital is immaterial. Ten depositors each deposit £100 in treasury notes with this bank. Its liabilities to the public are now £1,000. These ten depositors have business with each other and find it more convenient in many cases to write notes (cheques) to the banker, instructing him to adjust their several accounts in accordance with these business transactions, rather than to draw out cash and pay it over personally. After a little while, the banker notes that only about 10 per cent of his business is done in cash (in England it is only 0.7 of 1 per cent), the rest being merely book-keeping. At this point depositor No. 10, who is a manufacturer,

158

receives a large order for his product. Before he can deliver, he realises that he will have to pay out, in wages, salaries, and other expenses, considerably more "money" than he has at command. In this difficulty he consults his banker, who, having in mind the situation just outlined, agrees to allow him to draw from his account not merely his own £100, but an "overdraft" of £100, making £200 in all, in consideration of repayment in say, three months, of £102. This overdraft of £100 is a credit to the account of depositor No. 10, who can now draw £200.

The banker's liabilities to the public are now £1,100; none of the original depositors have had their credits of £100 each reduced by the transaction, nor were they consulted in regard to it; and it is absolutely correct to say that £100 of new money has been created by a stroke of the banker's pen.

Depositor No. 10 having, happily, obtained his overdraft, pays it out to his employees in wages and salaries. These wages and salaries, together with the banker's interest, all go into costs. All costs go into the price the public pays for its goods, and consequently, when depositor No. 10 repays his banker with £102 obtained from the public in exchange for his goods, and the banker, after placing £2, created by himself, to his profit and loss account, sets the £100 received against the phantom credit previously created, and cancels both of them; there are £100 worth more goods in the world which are immobilised—of which no one, not even the banker, except potentially, has the money equivalent. A short mathematical proof of this process is given in Appendix I, page 138.

There is, I think, little question that the true objective of the industrial system is the production and distribution of goods and services. Assuming this to be so, an examination of the existing arrangements with a view to discovering the causes of their partial failure, is involved.

The application of engineering methods to the production of goods and services has enabled one human unit to produce considerably more goods and services than are necessary for his own use. The application of mechanical power and improved process and organisation can tend only to increase the output per man-hour. It should be obvious, therefore, that a system by which purchasing power is distributed mainly through the agency of wages conflicts sharply with the physical reality involved in the fact that a decreasing number of persons tend to be involved in the production of the necessary amount of goods and services.

Before leaving this portion of the subject, however, it may be desirable to indicate the effect of raising or lowering wages considered as a component in the cost of unit production.

The money distributed in the production of of goods consists in wages and salaries. (Dividends are distributed subsequently to the sale of goods.) Since labour costs are not the only costs of production,

Labour costs are < prices,

$$\frac{costs}{prices} \text{ is } < 1.$$

If wages, that is to say, labour costs, are

reduced by an amount x, the ratio of purchasing power to prices is lessened

$$\frac{\text{costs}-x}{\text{prices}-x} \text{ is } < \frac{\text{costs}}{\text{prices}}$$

We can deduce, therefore, that lessening the item of labour costs in the total factory cost of an article reduces the capacity of the wage-earning portion of the population to buy the total volume of goods produced, although for a total amount of wages distributed the amount of goods produced is obviously greater.

Since it is generally recognised that the average dividend of an industrial undertaking distributed to the shareholders is very small compared to the amount distributed in wages and salaries, probably not averaging more than 3 per cent, we may be led to suspect that the reduction of the ratio of direct labour costs to total costs involves a principle of fundamental importance. This is so. If we take a cross-section of the flow of purchasing power delivered to the buying public in the form of wages, salaries, and dividends, and at the same moment take a cross-section of the flow of prices generated in the industrial system, we shall find that the latter cross-section is always greater than the former. This may be put as follows. All industrial payments may be divided into two groups.

Group A.—All payments made to individuals (wages, salaries, and dividends).

Group B.—All payments made to other organisations (raw materials, repayment of bank loans, and other non-personal costs).

Now the rate of flow of purchasing power to individuals is represented by A, but since all payments go into prices, the rate of flow of prices cannot be less than A plus B. Since A will not purchase A plus B, a proportion of the product at least equivalent to B must be distributed by a form of purchasing power which is not comprised in the descriptions grouped under A.

The explanation of this apparent anomaly is complex, but is in the main due to the fact that the buyer of goods is at one and the same time paying for the goods and repaying to the

163

banking system, via intermediate producers, the money which the industrial system borrowed from it but which the banking system created by means of a book-keeping transaction.

The repayment of bank loans in the industrial system may be considered as included in the balance of the payments made from one business organisation to another, that is to say, in Group B, as explained above.

On the assumption that the delivery of goods and services is the objective of the industrial system, it is obvious that the rate of flow of purchasing power should be equal to the rate of generation of prices. The existing financial arrangements make a crude effort to approximate this condition by issuing purchasing power to manufacturing organisations in the form of loans, which in turn the manufacturing organisations distribute in wages and salaries against future production. In other words, the existing financial system increasingly mortgages the future in order to sell the goods existing at present, the most recent and most obvious form of this practice being the instalment system of purchase. Since the financial system is in essence merely a book-keeping system, having for its proper objective something not very dissimilar to the "progress" department of a large factory, the defect in it which is disclosed by the preceding cursory examination is obviously capable of adjustment.

Bearing in mind the premise that the consumer should collectively have the financial means to exercise the full call on both the sum of actual production and the balance of potential production represented by unused plant and available labour and material, it is easy to see that under existing conditions prices ought to vary inversely as the rate of production. The difficulty involved in this is that producers would lose money, and to avoid this and to stimulate production some modification is necessary.

Reverting to the physical realities of the productive system, it can easily be seen that the true cost of a given programme of production is the consumption of all production over an equivalent period of time; that is to say, if P equals production and C equals consumption, and M equals money distributed for a given programme of production, the true cost of this programme of production is not M, but

$$M \times \frac{\int_{T_1}^{T_2} \frac{dC}{dt}\, dt}{\int_{T_1}^{T_2} \frac{dP}{dt}\, dt} = M \times \frac{\text{mean consumption rate for selected period}}{\text{mean production rate for selected period}}$$

In other words, the true cost of a programme of production is in general not the money cost, but considerably less than the money cost, and a given programme of production can be distributed to the buying public only if sold at its true cost.

Many methods will suggest themselves for putting into operation the foregoing principles. Articles might be sold at cost *plus* profit as at present, and a rebate to the purchaser be made through the banking system, representing the difference between the apparent cost and the true cost. The source from which this rebate would be made would be exactly the same source from which at present the banking system creates money out of nothing, that is to say a book entry based on the security of a country considered as a producing mechanism. No inflation is involved in such a process. Inflation consists in an expansion of the figures of money available accompanied by a corresponding rise in prices. The objective in this case being a fall of prices to bring them collectively within the buying range of the general public, any rise of prices would merely result in the use of a smaller amount of credit.

It will be realised from the foregoing analysis that a considerable increase in the total purchasing power is necessary to obtain a sufficient effective demand upon the possibilities of the modern industrial system. Having obtained this initial increase in effective demand, the problem of the distribution of the increase assumes manageable proportions. Merely to endeavour to reallocate the initially deficient amount of purchasing power by taxation, as at present, can only result in a serious curtailment of production.

INDEX

169

INDEX

170

171

173

175

INDEX

ABOUT THE AUTHOR

THE late Clifford Hugh Douglas, M.I.Mech.E., M.I.E.E., consulting engineer, economist, author, and founder of the Social Credit Movement, was born in 1879 and died in 1952. Among other posts which he held in his earlier years were those of engineer with the Canadian General Electric Company, Peterborough, Canada; Assistant Engineer, Lachine Rapids Hydraulic Construction, Deputy Chief Electrical Engineer, Buenos Aires and Pacific Railway; Chief Engineer and Manager in India, British Westinghouse Company; Assistant Superintendent, Royal Aircraft Factory, Farnborough (England). During the First World War he was a Major in the Royal Flying Corps and later in the R.A.F. (Reserve).

After retiring from his engineering career, he and his wife ran a small yacht-building yard on Southampton Water for several years. The combination of beauty with functional efficiency in a successfully designed racing yacht had a special appeal for him. When he lived in an old water mill in Hampshire he used the water wheel to turn a dynamo which lit and warmed the house as well as providing power for lathes and other tools. Later, when he moved to Scotland, many of his friends and followers remember helping to build his small hydroelectric power house, sited on the local burn which ran through his land. Since decentralisation of economic power was of the essence of his teaching, it should be put on record that he practised what he preached.

One of his most interesting jobs, just before the 1914 War, was that of conducting preliminary experimental work and preparing plans and specifications for the electrical work on the Post Office Tube in London, with later supervision of the installation of plant in what was to be one of the earliest examples of complete automation in the history of engineering. While there were no physical difficulties about the work, he used to get orders from time to time to slow it up and pay off the men. When the War came, however, he noticed that here was no longer any difficulty about getting money for anything the Government wanted.

It appears that he was sent to Farnborough in 1916 to sort out "a certain amount of muddle" in the Aircraft Factory's accounts, so that he had to go very carefully into the costing. This he did by introducing what were then known as "tabulating machines"—an approach which anticipated the much later use of computers, and which drew his attention to the much faster rate at which the factory was generating costs as compared with the rate at which it was distributing incomes in the form of wages and salaries. Could this be true of every factory or commercial business?

Douglas then collected information from over 100 large businesses in Great Britain, and found that, in every case except in businesses heading for bankruptcy, the total costs always exceeded the sums paid out in wages, salaries and dividends. It followed that only a part of the final product could be distributed through the incomes disbursed by its production, and, moreover, a diminishing part as industrial

181

processes lengthened and became more complex and increased the ratio of overheads to current wages. Unless this defect in monetary book-keeping were corrected (which in his view was perfectly practicable) the distribution of the remainder must depend increasingly on work in progress on future products (whether wanted or not) financed by loan credit, export credits, sales below cost leading to bankruptcies and centralisation of industrial power, or by consumer borrowing. The result must be predictably disastrous—in fact, the modern dilemma between mass-poverty through unemployment and growing inflation, debt and monopoly, with waste of human effort and the earth's resources to maintain "full employment", requiring continuous economic "growth" and economic warfare between nations leading towards military war.

This original engineer's approach, which regarded the monetary system much as Douglas, a former railway engineer, had regarded the ticket system, as a mere book-keeping convenience for the efficient distribution of the product, was completely alien and unacceptable to the economic theorists of the day. Only one Professor of Economics (Professor Irvine of Sydney) expressed agreement with it, and he resigned his post shortly afterwards. This general condemnation by the economists was, however, along two different and contradictory lines, viz.: 1. that the cost-income gap was an illusion due to Douglas's failure to realise that the costs all represented sums paid out at a previous date as wages, salaries, etc.—ignoring the time factor which was the essence of his analysis; and, 2. that it was, on the contrary, a glimpse of the obvious, of no significance whatever, since this was the immutable way in which the monetary and economic system must work for the stimulation of new production and the maintenance of the level of employment—i.e. ignoring Douglas's radically different objective of production for the consumers' use and not for "employment" or other monetary objectives.

When the Great Depression of the 1930's grimly confirmed Douglas's diagnosis and gave him a world-wide reputation and following, his critics explained that he had mistaken a temporary lapse for a permanent defect in the monetary system; but subsequent events have, by now, so continuously fulfilled his predictions that this criticism is no longer credible. Despite rejection by the Economic Establishment of the day, Douglas was called upon to give evidence before the Canadian Banking Enquiry in 1923 and the Macmillan Committee in 1930, and undertook several World Tours in which he addressed many gatherings, especially in Canada, Australia and New Zealand, and also at the World Engineering Congress in Tokyo in 1929. In 1935 he gave an important address before the King of Norway and the British Minister at the Oslo Merchants' Club, and in the same year he was appointed Chief Reconstruction Adviser to the "United Farmers" Government of the Province of Alberta, Canada, which later in the year elected the first Government to bear the title "Social Credit". The Canadian Federal Government, however, frustrated all attempts to implement Douglas's advice by disallowing the legislation, some of which was passed, and disallowed, twice; after which, although the Party remained in power for over 30 years, it progressively abandoned the principles on which it was first elected. It should be placed on historical record, as a precedent, that two "provincial dividends" of little more than token value, were nevertheless paid at one period to the citizens of the Province, and that, while still acting under the advice of Douglas's representative, the province paid its way without further borrowing, and drastically reduced the Provincial debt.

This diversion of Douglas's ideas into the dead-end of Party politics has received far more publicity than the original and experimental approach to politics which is signposted in his later speeches and writings from 1934 onwards, notably in his five major speeches in England: *The Nature of Democracy, The Tragedy of Human Effort, The Approach to Reality, The Policy of a Philosophy*, and *Realistic Constitutionalism.* In 1934 a Social Credit Secretariat was formed under his Chairmanship, which started an Electoral Campaign involving the use of the vote for purposes desired by electors rather than by Parliament or the political Parties. This was was followed by a highly successful Local Objectives Campaign along similar non-party lines, and a Lower Rates and Assessments Campaign which saved the British ratepayers many millions of pounds without loss of services, by reducing loan charges. The Second World War put an end to these activities on an organised national scale, and dispersed them, with the Social Credit Movement, into a decentralised force, better adapted to the present crisis of World centralisation.

In the final phase of his life, roughly from 1939 to his death in 1952, Douglas consolidated his ideas in depth, contrasting very clearly the philosophy which underlies them with that which activates the Monopoly of Credit. Although the best known of them, which have already exercised considerable influence in the World, lie in the economic sphere: the concepts of real credit, the increment of association and the cultural inheritance, and the proposals of the Natonal Dividend and the Just or Compensated Price—his political ideas, though as yet little known, are if anything of greater importance. They were always worked out

186

with a characteristic practicality, taking account of the feed-back from the course of events. No one else has thrown so much light on the true nature of democracy, as distinct from the numerical product of the ballot box; on the need for decentralised control of policy and hierarchical control of administration; on the freedom to choose one thing at a time, on the right to contract out, on the Voters' Policy and the Voters' Veto. In his last address, given in London to the Constitutional Research Association in 1947, he put forward his last proposal for the rehabilitation of democracy: the Responsible Vote, in which the financial consequences of his open electoral choice would be, for a time, differentially paid for by the voter in proportion to his income—a literally revolutionary suggestion which demands an inversion of current ideas about anonymous, irresponsible, numerical voting.

Hugh Gaitskell, a former Leader of the Labour Party, once sarcastically described Douglas as "a religious rather than a scientific reformer". Perhaps he was more right than he knew! It may be that Douglas's thinking on the subjects of philosophy, policy and religion, and the special meaning he gave to those words, will turn out to be his most valuable contribution to the restoring of the link between religious belief and the principles which govern Society. In his view, a "philosophy", i.e. a conception of the universe, always expresses itself as a "policy"—a distinctive long-term course of action directed towards ends determined by that "philosophy". "Religion" (from the Latin *religare*, to bind back) is not just a set of beliefs such as are expressed in the Christian creeds (which constitute a "philosophy") but is precisely the "binding back" of these ideas to the reality of our lives, not only individually, but in the political and economic relationships of our society.

The policies of centralisation and monopoly now being imposed upon the World through the closely related agencies of Finance-Capitalism and Marxist Socialism derive from a "philosophy" fundamentally different from, and opposed to, that of Trinitarian Christianity, which was, however imperfectly, expressed in our Constitution, our Common Law, and the

188

progress towards personal freedom which had been made, especially, in Britain and the Commonwealth. At the time Douglas first put forward his ideas and proposals for carrying forward this traditional policy to its next stage, its Christian basis could be taken for granted as mere "common sense". Now, that can no longer be taken for granted, and it has become necessary consciously to distinguish the policies at work in our Society, and to relate them to the fundamental beliefs which gave rise to them. In this sense, therefore, "Social Credit" is the social policy of a Christian "philosophy"; and before the end of his life, its founder made this explicit, rather than, as in its beginnings, implicit.

After reading this challenging book, why not order additional copies for your relations and friends.

Additional copies of this book and a complete list of other available works by C. H. Douglas may be obtained by writing to one of the following:

UNITED KINGDOM
 Bloomfield Books,
 26 Meadow Lane, SUDBURY,
 Suffolk, ENGLAND, CO10 6TD.

AUSTRALIA
 Heritage Publications,
 273 Little Collins Street, MELBOURNE,
 Victoria, AUSTRALIA, 3000.

CANADA
 Canadian Intelligence Publications,
 Box 130, FLESHERTON,
 Ontario, CANADA, NOC 1EO.

NEW ZEALAND
 Conservative Publications,
 P.O. Box 736, TAURANGA,
 NEW ZEALAND.

SOUTH AFRICA
 Dolphin Press (Pty) Ltd.,
 P.O. Box 1564, KRUGERSDORP,
 Transvaal, SOUTH AFRICA, 1740.

Printed by G. M. Jerrold & Co., Chalford Hill, Stroud, Glos.